The Best of The Mailbox®
Bulletin Boards Book 2

Table of Contents

About This Book

Packed with loads of our most popular bulletin boards for primary teachers, ***The Best of* The Mailbox® *Bulletin Boards—Book 2*** is the perfect resource for creating an inviting classroom! Inside you'll find more than 100 motivating and easy-to-create displays compiled from *The Mailbox®* line of magazines and books.

Organized by season, this handy resource includes displays for fall, winter, and spring and a special collection for any day of the year. A wide array of patterns accompany the boards, saving you valuable time in creating and setting up your displays. Use the boards to supplement instruction, manage your classroom, and display student work. ***The Best of* The Mailbox® *Bulletin Boards— Book 2*** is the best resource for an eye-catching classroom!

Managing Editors: Kelli L. Gowdy, Allison E. Ward
Editor at Large: Diane Badden
Copy Editors: Tazmen Carlisle, Amy Kirtley-Hill, Kristy Parton, Debbie Shoffner, Cathy Edwards Simrell
Cover Artist: Clevell Harris
Art Coordinators: Theresa Lewis Goode, Stuart Smith
Artists: Pam Crane, Chris Curry, Shane Freeman, Theresa Lewis Goode, Clevell Harris, Ivy L. Koonce, Clint Moore, Greg D. Rieves, Rebecca Saunders, Barry Slate, Stuart Smith, Donna K. Teal
The Mailbox® Books.com: Judy P. Wyndham (MANAGER); Jennifer Tipton Bennett (DESIGNER/ARTIST); Karen White (INTERNET COORDINATOR); Paul Fleetwood, Xiaoyun Wu (SYSTEMS)

President, The Mailbox Book Company™: Joseph C. Bucci
Director of Book Planning and Development: Chris Poindexter
Curriculum Director: Karen P. Shelton
Book Development Managers: Cayce Guiliano, Elizabeth H. Lindsay, Thad McLaurin
Editorial Planning: Kimberley Bruck (DIRECTOR); Debra Liverman, Sharon Murphy, Susan Walker (TEAM LEADERS)
Editorial and Freelance Management: Karen A. Brudnak; Sarah Hamblet, Hope Rodgers (EDITORIAL ASSISTANTS)
Editorial Production: Lisa K. Pitts (TRAFFIC MANAGER); Lynette Dickerson (TYPE SYSTEMS); Mark Rainey (TYPESETTER)
Librarian: Dorothy C. McKinney

www.themailbox.com

Fall

Any way you slice it, this scrumptious display makes a big impression! Give each student a copy of the **seed pattern** (page 80) and have her illustrate her favorite summer memory. Then have each child glue her cutout on slightly larger black paper and trim the paper to create a border. Invite each child to tell her classmates about her summer memory; then mount the projects on a giant slice of watermelon.

Kristin McLaughlin—Gr. 1, Daniel Boone Area School District, Boyertown, PA

Enlist your students' help in creating this "sun-sational" back-to-school display. Ask each student to bring to school a post-card, snapshot, or other souvenir from a favorite summer happening. Have each child dictate a sentence about his summer experience for you to copy on a sentence strip. Enlarge the **map pattern** (page 81); then mount the corresponding sentences and memorabilia on a display like the one shown. Use yarn lengths to show where each event took place.

Vicki O'Neal—Gr. 2, Lincoln Elementary, Baxter Springs, KS

Reap a crop of student goals at this ever-growing display! Display a backdrop, title, and tractor-driving character similar to the ones shown. You will also need one seed packet and one wooden craft stick per child. On the first day of school, ask each student to write her goals for the school year and to explain how she plans to achieve them. Then mount each student's writing onto the display as shown.

Diane Afferton—Gr. 3, Chapin School, Princeton, NJ

Focus in on a great school year with this eye-catching display! To create the giant-size camera, cover a bulletin board with black paper; then use poster board, foil, and paper scraps to create a camera lens, viewfinder, flash, shutter button, and other desired details. From white paper, cut a circle that is slightly smaller than the camera lens. Visually divide the circle so that each child has a section in which to illustrate and personalize his self-likeness. Mount the completed circle inside the camera lens.

adapted from an idea by Karen Kruger, Klondike Lane Elementary, Louisville, KY

If you're looking for a "tree-mendous" back-to-school display, try this one! Mount one or more tree cutouts and a suitable title. Make a class supply of the **apple pattern** (page 82). Give a pattern to each student and have him write his name and a short paragraph about himself. Then have each child glue his cutout on slightly larger red paper, trim the paper to create a border, and attach a green paper stem. Have students read their paragraphs aloud before mounting the projects on the display.

Annamaria Vitucci Walters—Gr. 3, St. Joseph School–Fullerton, Baltimore, MD

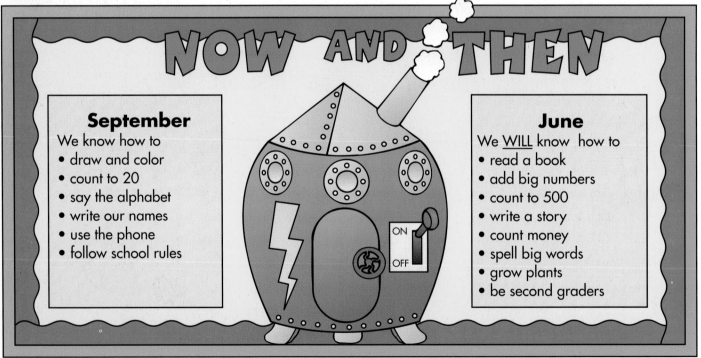

What does the future hold for your students? To find out the answer to that question, go right to the source! Mount the title and a large **time machine pattern** (page 83). Then, under your students' guidance, prepare two lists: one that details what the students know right now and one that details what the students plan to know at the end of the school year. Showcase the completed lists at the display. The future looks bright!

Whitney Sherman—Gr. 1, Seven Pines Elementary School, Sandston, VA

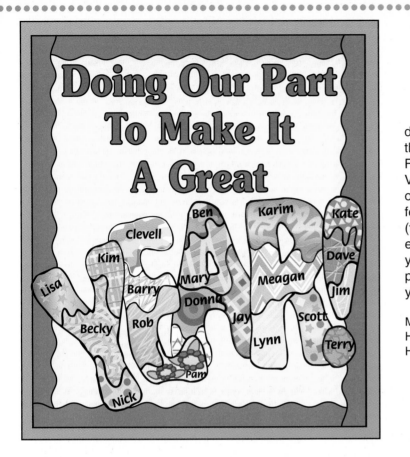

Great things are created with teamwork, and this display is a perfect example! Mount a border and the phrase "Doing Our Part to Make It a Great." From poster board, cut large letters to spell "YEAR." Visually divide the letter cutouts into a class supply of puzzle pieces; then label each piece for a different student. Code the back of each letter cutout (for easy reassembly) before cutting it apart. Have each child decorate his puzzle piece. Then, with your youngsters' help, assemble and mount the puzzle pieces as shown. It's going to be a great year!

Mary Jo Kampschnieder—Gr. 2
Howells Community Catholic School
Howells, NE

This travel display is quite a sight! Make a class supply of the **car pattern** (page 84). Give each student a copy of the pattern and ask her to ponder the places she visited over the summer as she personalizes, colors, and cuts out her car. Then have her write and illustrate a story about one place she visited. Display the students' stories and cars as shown. Invite students to continue their travels by reading about their classmates' trips!

adapted from an idea by Angie Kelley—Gr. 3, Weaver Elementary School, Anniston, AL

Show students that each of them holds a key to success! Enlist their help in naming behaviors that unlock positive learning experiences. Next, have each child personalize and cut out a large **key pattern** (page 84), glue the cutout to a colorful rectangle, and label the rectangle with her goal for a positive year. Mount the projects and title. There you have it, a colorful reminder of what is key for a great year!

Kathie Eckelkamp—Gr. 2, Most Precious Blood School, St. Louis, MO

Dispense a colorful classroom welcome with this hallway display. A student uses assorted arts-and-crafts supplies to create her self-likeness on a colorful paper circle. Enlarge the **gumball base pattern** (page 85) onto colorful paper. Mount the resulting cutout, the student projects, and the title. For the dome, tape a large circle of clear plastic over the projects. By gum, that's a cute display!

Jo Fryer—Gr. 1
Kildeer Countryside School
Long Grove, IL

We're Bananas About School!

Jackson Ms. Petges Seth Ami Tyrone Carmen Eugene Alex Dylan Tanya Kyle Jessica Jordan Adam Allison Christopher Lizzie

If you want your youngsters to go bananas over school, here's the perfect display! On a paper-covered bulletin board, mount a large **monkey and tree pattern** (page 86) and the title as shown. Then, using colorful markers, have the students write their names on the display. When the project is finished, serve each child one-half of a banana. Then invite your youngsters to talk about their expectations for the new school year.

Susie Petges—Gr. 2, St. Dennis School, Lockport, IL

Check Me Out!

Create miles of smiles with this back-to-school display. Cover a bulletin board with white paper. A student uses assorted arts-and-crafts supplies to create her likeness on a construction paper oval. Then she mounts her likeness and precut letters spelling "ME" on a colorful rectangle. Display the projects in a checkerboard pattern, leaving room for the title near the top. You can count on plenty of students, parents, and staff members checking out this display!

Linda Macke—Gr. 3, John F. Kennedy Elementary, Kettering, OH

Start the year off right with a bushel of good behavior tips. Mount the title and basket as shown. Using the **apple patterns** (page 86), make and cut out a supply of yellow, green, and red apple shapes. Ask students to brainstorm tips for good behavior; then write the youngsters' ideas on the chalkboard. Later select and copy several of their ideas on the apple cutouts. Mount the programmed apples along with a couple of adorable worm cutouts as shown.

Sandra Daugherty—Grs. 1 & 2, Stinking Creek School, LaFollette, TN

Apple Adjectives

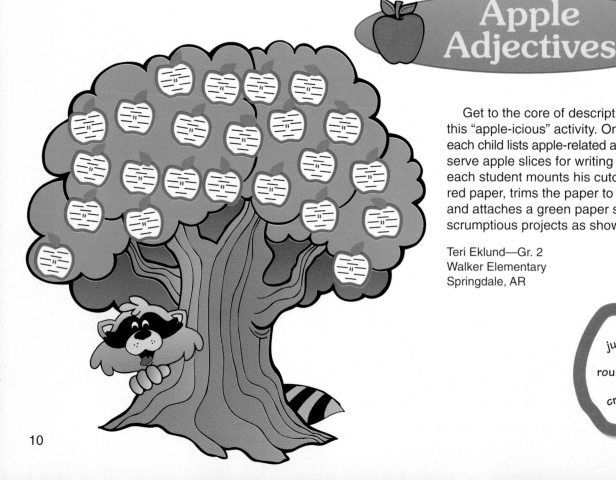

Get to the core of descriptive adjectives with this "apple-icious" activity. On a provided cutout, each child lists apple-related adjectives. If desired, serve apple slices for writing inspiration. Then each student mounts his cutout on slightly larger red paper, trims the paper to create a border, and attaches a green paper stem. Display the scrumptious projects as shown.

Teri Eklund—Gr. 2
Walker Elementary
Springdale, AR

juicy crisp
red
round tasty
crunchy fresh
shiny

Fall is a perfect time to snuggle up with a quilt-making project. Each student creates a fall scene on a white paper plate using paper scraps, glue, and other desired supplies. Mount the projects on colorful squares and display as shown. Use a marker to draw stitches. When each new season rolls around, have each student design a new scene for the quilt. Now that's a year-round display that's easy to get comfortable with!

Linda Parris—Gr. 1, West Hills Elementary, Knoxville, TN

Make penmanship practice a daily goal at this interactive bulletin board! Post the title and **cheerleader and football player patterns** (pages 87 and 88), a laminated poster with handwriting lines, student directions, a supply of laminated handwriting paper, and a Press-On Pocket containing a cloth and several wipe-off markers. Use one marker to write a cursive letter on the poster. Each day students head to the practice field to fine-tune their cursive writing skills!

Kelly W. Mize, Gr. 2, Heritage Christian School, Huntsville, AL

If you're planning to invite your students' grandparents and/or older adult friends into the classroom, this display is a must! On a 3½-inch white circle, have each child illustrate one or more grandparents or older adult friends. Then have each child glue her project on a blue construction paper **ribbon pattern** (page 89). Mount the completed projects on a display like the one shown.

Beth Vander Kolk—Gr. 1, The Potter's House, Grand Rapids, MI

Celebrate National Grandparents Day with this display honoring your students' grandparents and older adult friends! Ask each child to illustrate herself enjoying the company of her grandparent or older friend. Mount the completed projects along with the **squirrel pattern** (page 90) for everyone to enjoy!

Mary Jo Kampschnieder—Gr. 2, Howells Community Catholic, Howells, NE

Look Who's Hiding In The Pumpkin Patch!

Here's an open house display that's a guaranteed crowd-pleaser! Each student cuts a pumpkin shape from orange paper. On her resulting cutout, she writes three or four self-describing clues followed by the question "Who am I?" Tape a snapshot of the student near the bottom of her pumpkin; then cover the snapshot with a flap of orange paper. Display the projects as shown. During open house challenge parents to find their children in the pumpkin patch!

adapted from an idea by Leigh-Ann Hensal, Lockport, NY

Barn Dance!

Head down to the barn for a little foot-stompin' fun! To make a three-dimensional scarecrow, stuff a pair of child-size bib overalls and a shirt with crumpled newspaper. Add yarn hands and feet. To make the head, stitch and stuff a piece of burlap; then add hair, facial features, and a hat. Assemble and display the scarecrow holding a paper violin. Then, using only construction paper and glue, each child creates a dancing scarecrow.

Cheryl Hinschberger, Challenger Elementary School, Thief River Falls, MN

The Cream Of The Crop!

Harvest a bumper crop of self-esteem at this manipulative display. Using the **corn patterns** along with an enlarged **scarecrow pattern** (page 91), duplicate for each child a yellow ear of corn and two green corn husks. A child writes his name and why he feels special on his ear of corn. Next he cuts out his patterns, stacks the husks atop the ear of corn, and pokes a brad through the black dots, joining the three cutouts. Display the projects as shown. Let the harvest begin!

Jacqueline L. Jerke—Title I Reading And Math, Wynot Public Schools, Wynot, NE

This seaworthy display encourages critical thinking. Prior to investigating the voyages of Columbus, each child colors a **ship pattern** and **sail pattern** (page 93), cuts out the patterns, and glues them to opposite ends of a craft stick as shown. Then she uses a pushpin to display her completed project. Revisit the display throughout your study, each time allowing students to keep or change their votes. Encourage plenty of discussion and accept all responses. What a fleet!

Robin Kopecky—Title I Reading Consultant, Lake Louise School, Palatine, IL

Invite students "haunting" for good books to peek inside these windows (if they dare)! Have each child write the title and author of a favorite book on provided paper and then illustrate a memorable scene from the book. Staple yellow paper atop each child's project and then display the projects on a spooky house cutout. Boo!

Tiffany L. Gosseen
Hopkins, MO

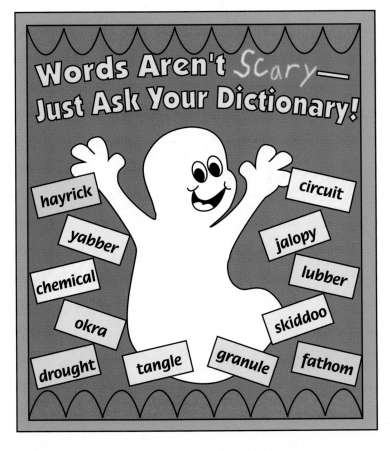

Scare up some dictionary interest at this seasonal display! Mount a **ghost pattern** (page 94) and the title. Place a dictionary and a supply of word cards nearby. Each day ask one student to copy a *scary* (unfamiliar) dictionary entry word onto a word card. Post the student's word card, and help the student read the word and its dictionary meaning aloud. Discuss the word and invite students to try using it in sentences. Review the other words posted at the display too. Gee, words aren't scary—they're "spook-tacular"!

Vicki O'Neal—Gr. 2
Lincoln Elementary
Baxter Springs, KS

Scare up some great student work and a whole lot of fun at this seasonal display. Mount the title, a **ghost pattern** (page 95), the caption "Bump Board!" and samples of exceptional student work. When the display is full, the bumping begins. Each student whose work is chosen for the display gets to bump another paper off the board. You can count on plenty of "boo-tiful" work during October!

Judy Knight—Gr. 3, Day Elementary, San Angelo, TX

Great gobblers! Have you ever seen such flawless tail feathers? Mount the title and an enlarged **turkey pattern** (page 96). Copy a supply of the **feather pattern** (page 97) onto colored paper. Each week, every child who aces the spelling test mounts her paper on a feather cutout. Keep adding these feathers to the bird throughout November and two things are certain to happen: Spelling scores will improve, and you'll have a one-of-a-kind gobbler on display!

Gale Kotner—Gr. 2
Southern View Elementary School
Springfield, IL

This grinning gobbler has a tail full of questions for students to answer! Number and program a supply of **feather patterns** (page 97) with seasonal questions like "What is a female turkey called?" and "What ocean did the Pilgrims cross?" Mount the feathers, an enlarged **turkey pattern** (page 96), and the title as shown. Near the display provide books that contain the answers to the posted questions. Research has never been more fun!

Julie Plowman—Gr. 3, Adair-Casey Elementary, Adair, IA

This Thanksgiving create a feast for the eyes! Mount the title, an enlarged **turkey pattern** (page 98), and a length of bulletin-board paper titled "Look What We've Read!" Then, under your students' guidance, list book titles that you've read to the class and titles that the class has read. Ask the students to vote for their favorite book from the list, and attach a blue ribbon beside the title that earns the most votes. Gobble, gobble!

adapted from an idea by
Robin Kopecky—Grs. 1–3
Lake Louise School
Palatine, IL

Enlist your youngsters' help in creating this unique rendering of the first Thanksgiving. To make the table, tape a series of boxes end to end and cover the resulting shape with bulletin-board paper. Set this dinner table atop a bookcase or table that you've positioned below the display. Mount the title and a series of student-created dinner guests as shown. Showcase pumpkins, squash, dried corn, and other appropriate items on the dinner table. Now that's a feast!

Linda Valentino—Gr. 2, Minisink Valley Elementary, Slate Hill, NY

When November arrives, have students brush up on nouns as they harvest a bounty of thankfulness. Enlarge the **turkey pattern** (page 99). As students brainstorm people, places, and things for which they are thankful, write the corresponding nouns on the chalkboard. Ask each child to choose one noun, then copy and illustrate the noun. After a child shares his completed project with the class, he mounts his work in the appropriate noun category on the display.

Margaret Leyen—Gr. 2, Pineview Elementary, Iowa Falls, IA

Winter

Warm students up to wintry writing and create this toasty display! Post a student-generated list of adjectives that describe mittens or wintry weather. Give each student a copy of the **mitten patterns** (page 100). A student decorates the blank pattern; then she writes a descriptive poem or paragraph about her decorated mitten on the lined pattern. Mount the mitten projects and the title as shown. Invite students to take the chill off winter by reading their classmates' mitten-related writing!

Jennifer Balogh-Joiner—Gr. 2, Franklin Elementary, Franklin, NJ

Your students will have a ball creating this winter wonderland! Each student chooses a winter scene from a coloring book or a similar resource; then she secures a clear transparency atop the scene. Next, using appropriate markers, she colors the transparency as if she were coloring the picture. Mount the student artwork on a bulletin board covered with aluminum foil.

Linda B. Vaughn—Gr. 2 & Mary Jo White—Gr. 2 Assistant, Franklin Elementary School, Mt. Airy, NC

Check out this versatile display! Mount a large, kid-pleasing **bunny pattern** (page 101). When you're studying Antarctica, adorn the bunny with the winter **hat pattern** (page 101), add the title shown, and display penguin-related student work. For an ocean theme, use the title "An Undersea Adventure"; then adorn the bunny with scuba diving headgear and display ocean-related student work. The possibilities are endless!

Jill Krueger—Gr. 2, Thousand Oaks Elementary, San Antonio, TX

This eye-catching scene is effortless to assemble. Drape a length of fabric or a bedsheet across the top of a bulletin board (securing it at each corner and in the middle) to make a curtain for your "window." Then, using white chalk and scraps of construction paper, have each student create a winter scene on dark blue paper. Mount the completed projects atop slightly larger pieces of black paper; then attach black-paper windowpanes. Ooooooh! What a sight!

Katie McLean—Gr. 1, Thomasville Elementary School, Thomasville, AL

Has Frosty gone vogue? After making a class supply of the **snowperson pattern** (page 102), have students color half sheets of graph paper by alternating two or more colors of crayons or markers. On the backs of these papers, have students draw and cut out mittens, buttons, scarves, and hats. Finally, have students attach the colorful clothing to a snowperson. Mount the completed projects on a display like the one shown. Totally cool!

Leslie A. Hoffman—Gr. 1, St. Michael's Elementary, Hastings, NE

Promote creative thinking with a one-of-a-kind winter wonderland! To make a penguin, a child completes the sentence starter and signs his name on a **penguin pattern** (page 103). Then he colors the penguin and cuts it out. Next, he fashions winter wear from wallpaper, construction paper, or fabric scraps and glues it on his cutout. Showcase the projects and invite students to ponder the penguins' cool thoughts.

adapted from an idea by Lisa Dorsey—Gr. 2, Garland, TX

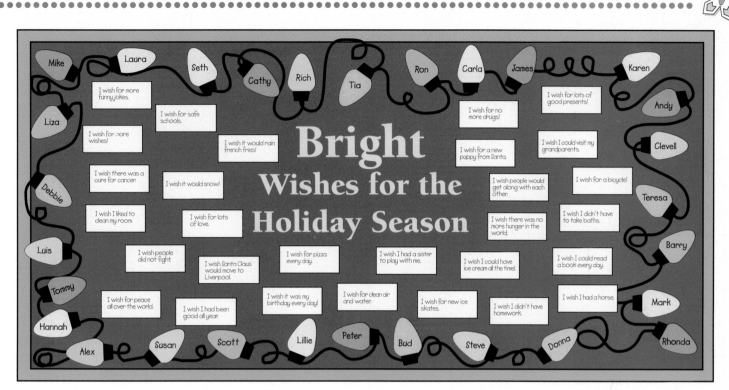

Light up the holiday season with goodwill wishes! On provided paper, each child writes a wish that will bring happiness to many people. Then he personalizes and cuts out a colorful holiday **lightbulb pattern** (page 103) and glues a three-inch square paper base to it. Mount the title and student projects. Use curling ribbon or curled strips of paper to connect the holiday lights. The season definitely looks bright!

Connie Todd—Title I Reading and Math, St. Aloysius Elementary School, East Liverpool, OH

Deck a wall (or hall!) with holiday traditions! Each student illustrates a favorite family tradition from this time of year on a seven-inch square of white paper, glues her illustration on a nine-inch square of black paper, and writes her family name on a 2" x 5" paper strip. Showcase the projects along with an enlarged **camera pattern** (page 104) and invite each child to share additional details about her family's tradition with the class. Happy holidays!

Catherine Broome, Melbourne Beach, FL

Looking for an "a-door-able" holiday display? Try this! Mount a large cookie jar cutout on your classroom door; then have each child decorate a **gingerbread cookie pattern** (page 105). Mount the projects as shown. How sweet it is!

Catherine Broome—Gr. 1
Forked River, NJ

Gifts Of The Season, Straight From The Heart

The gifts on this sleigh come straight from the heart! Seat students in a circle and give each child a large sheet of construction paper bearing his name. On your signal, each child passes his paper to the right. Then he signs the paper he is given and writes a positive note about the classmate who is named. Continue in this manner until each child receives his original paper. After each student reads the gifts he's been given, have him fold his paper in half and decorate it to resemble a holiday package. Display the gifts along with enlarged copies of the **birds and sleigh patterns** (page 106) throughout the holiday season.

adapted from ideas by M. J. Owen—Gr. 3, Baty Elementary, Del Valle, TX, and Denise Lapine—Special Education, Rockwell Elementary School, Nedrow, NY

Looking For A Helper

		N			
Brianne	Thomas		Erin		Victor
Alyssa	Joey		Jacob		Lali
W Michael				Eric	E
Lisa	Patrick		Pablo		Annie
Jessie	Maggie	S	Karen		Paul

Reinforce cardinal directions with this clever helper display. Visually divide a bulletin board into fourths, label the cardinal directions, and mount a seasonal picture in each quadrant. For each student, post a name card that is above, below, or beside a picture or another card. Each day identify a helper by citing a clue like "The name of today's helper is east of the dreidel." Each season or month, replace the pictures and rearrange the cards. To up the challenge, add intermediate directions too!

Vicki Neilon—Gr. 2, Antietam Elementary School, Lake Ridge, VA

Top-Notch Holiday Wishes!

I wish a happy holiday for everyone.

I wish for more wishes!

I wish for world peace.

I wish for no more drugs.

I wish for a new puppy.

I wish for lots of fun.

I wish for Kindness and love.

I wish for lots of food.

I wish that my daddy will get well.

I wish for no more Killing.

I wish for a house.

I wish for lots of candy.

I wish for snow.

I wish for a baby brother.

This seasonal display will have your youngsters spinning with holiday wishes! Mount the title, an enlarged **dreidel pattern** (page 107), and a dreidel path made from yarn. On a paper strip, each student writes his wish for the holiday season. Encourage students to consider wishes that could bring happiness to many people. Mount the students' wishes for all to read.

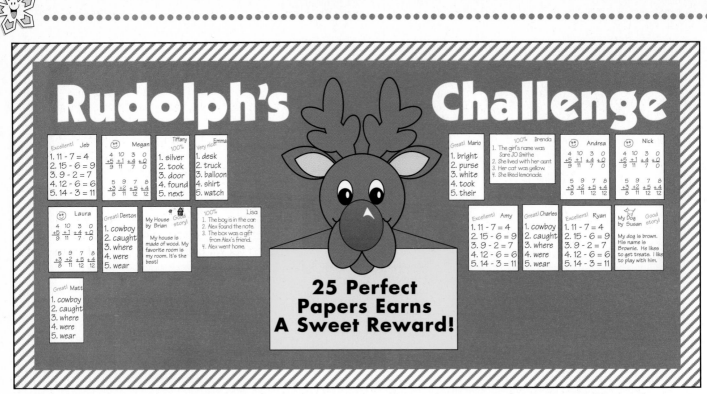

Rudolph's Challenge

25 Perfect Papers Earns A Sweet Reward!

Excellent! Jeb
1. 11 - 7 = 4
2. 15 - 6 = 9
3. 9 - 2 = 7
4. 12 - 6 = 6
5. 14 - 3 = 11

Megan
4 10 3 0
+5 +1 +4 +0
9 11 7 0

5 9 7 8
+3 +3 +5 +4
8 11 12 12

Tiffany
100%
1. silver
2. took
3. door
4. found
5. next

Very nice! Emma
1. desk
2. truck
3. balloon
4. shirt
5. watch

Great! Mario
1. bright
2. purse
3. white
4. took
5. their

100% Brenda
1. The girl's name was Sara JO Smithe.
2. She lived with her aunt.
3. Her cat was yellow.
4. She liked lemonade.

Andrea
4 10 3 0
+5 +1 +4 +0
9 11 7 0

5 9 7 8
+3 +3 +5 +4
8 11 12 12

Nick
4 10 3 0
+5 +1 +4 +0
9 11 7 0

5 9 7 8
+3 +3 +5 +4
8 11 12 12

Laura
4 10 3 0
+5 +1 +4 +0
9 11 7 0

5 9 7 8
+3 +2 +5 +4
8 11 12 12

Great! Denton
1. cowboy
2. caught
3. where
4. were
5. wear

My House by Brian
Good story!
My house is made of wood. My favorite room is my room. It's the best!

100% Lisa
1. The boy is in the car.
2. Alex found the note.
3. The box was a gift from Alex's friend.
4. Alex went home.

Excellent! Amy
1. 11 - 7 = 4
2. 15 - 6 = 9
3. 9 - 2 = 7
4. 12 - 6 = 6
5. 14 - 3 = 11

Great! Charles
1. cowboy
2. caught
3. where
4. were
5. wear

Excellent! Ryan
1. 11 - 7 = 4
2. 15 - 6 = 9
3. 9 - 2 = 7
4. 12 - 6 = 6
5. 14 - 3 = 11

My Dog by Susan
Good story!
My dog is brown. His name is Brownie. He likes to get treats. I like to play with him.

Great! Matt
1. cowboy
2. caught
3. where
4. were
5. wear

Let Rudolph lead the way to super student work! Mount a large **Rudolph pattern** (page 108), a sign that describes a class goal, and the title. If desired, tape an inflated balloon to Rudolph's nose. Make a supply of the **awards** (page 108) and cut them out; then attach an individually wrapped, red candy nose to each one. When the posted goal is met, return each paper with an award stapled to it. Then challenge the class to meet the goal again. Now that's a display that will go down in history!

Julie Plowman—Gr. 3, Adair-Casey Elementary, Adair, IA

A ngel | B ell | C andy Cane | D rum | E lf | F ood | G ingerbread
H olly | I cicles | J olly Santa | Our Christmas Quilt | K ing | L ove | M ittens
N utcracker | O rnament | P resents | Q uilt | R udolph | S tar | T ree

Deck your wall with this student-made Christmas quilt! To make his quilt patch, a student draws, colors, and cuts out a seasonal noun that represents the alphabet letter he has chosen. Then he mounts his cutout on a red or green rectangle. Label and mount the quilt patches in alphabetical order, inserting a title patch in the center. Use a marker or paint pen to draw stitches around the projects. Happy holidays!

Shirley J. Mitchell—Gr. 2, Erieview Elementary School, Avon Lake, OH

Let's Give Santa A Hand!

Your little ones will be eager to lend a hand in creating this seasonal display! Mount a jolly Santa face without his beard; then enlist your students in tracing and cutting out their hand shapes from black, white, and red paper. Use the resulting cutouts to form Santa's hat, suit, beard, belt, and boots. Add his gloves, a belt buckle, and a knob for his hat. To make Santa's list, give each student a narrow length of paper on which to write one way that he has been good during the past year. Then mount the students' work end-to-end on a strip of red paper and display the resulting list with Santa. Ho! Ho! Ho! Here comes Santa!

Pam Scott—Gr. 1
Brookdale Elementary
Macon, GA

Dear Santa,

I helped my mom. Love, Jill

I was nice to my brother. Love, Ryan

I tried really hard at school. Love, Alex

I ate all my vegetables. Love, Ryan

I made my own bed. Love, Keesha

I kept my room clean. Love, Eva

I improved in math. Love, Jamal

Create a spectacular sight this season with star-studded greenery! Copy onto green paper the **star pattern** (page 109) to make a class supply. Each student cuts out a pattern. Then she centers and glues a snapshot of herself on her cutout, making sure that one point of the star is directly above her picture. Each student then decorates her star as desired. Provide glitter pens, sequins, rickrack, pom-poms, and other arts-and-crafts supplies for this purpose. Be sure to fashion a star yourself! Then mount the completed projects as shown. Happy holidays!

Renee Fehr—Grs. 1 & 2
Westmoreland Elementary
Westmoreland, KS

Happy Holidays!

Deck your display with these quiet, little Christmas mice! Duplicate onto gray construction paper the **mouse patterns** (page 109) to make a class supply. Mount the banners and holly as shown; then attach the student-made mice. To make a mouse, a student cuts out the patterns and glues the ears to the body. She attaches a tiny, pink pom-pom nose and a spiraled pipe cleaner tail. Then she adds two black eyes. Shhh!

Alice Bertels—Special Education
Crestview Elementary
Topeka, KS

Celebrate the joy of giving of one's own self. Copy the **ornament patterns** (page 110) onto construction paper to make an ornament for each child. Write a student-generated list of free gift ideas on the chalkboard. Have each child decorate one holiday ornament. Collect the ornaments, label the back of each with an idea from the list, and mount them on the tree. Each day remove a project from the tree, read its inscription, and ask students to "give" the gift of the day. Plan ahead so that on the last school day prior to vacation, the final project is removed from the tree. Redisplay the daily gift suggestions as shown.

Jane M. Smith—Gr. 1, Green Mountain, IA

LEARNING SCORES!

My name is ___Allen___
This year I have learned how to write in cursive!
I am also learning how to multiply. I can spell
sandwich, Florida, and tackle. I can spell bats
are not really blind. I learned that spiders have
eight legs. I also learned that Ms. Hallman
has a sweet tooth.

Spotlight your youngsters' winning plays of the season! A student completes a copy of the **football pattern** (page 111) and cuts out the football shape. Then he glues his cutout onto a 9" x 12" sheet of brown construction paper and trims the brown paper to create a border. Display the projects as shown. Now that's a midseason game plan guaranteed to boost self-esteem!

Bernadette Hallman—Gr. 3
Annunciation Catholic School
Middleburg, FL

My resolution for 2004 is to practice my reading words each day.

Sarah

Students will have a ball drafting cool resolutions for the new year! Have each child write one goal for the new year in the center of a six-inch doily and then tape a four-inch doily atop his writing so that a flap is created. Give each child a second four-inch doily (for a snowpal's head), two twigs (for arms), and access to supplies so he can complete his snowpal. Display the projects on a snowy backdrop like the one shown. Happy New Year!

Kim Castro—Gr. 1, Engelwood Elementary School, Orlando, FL

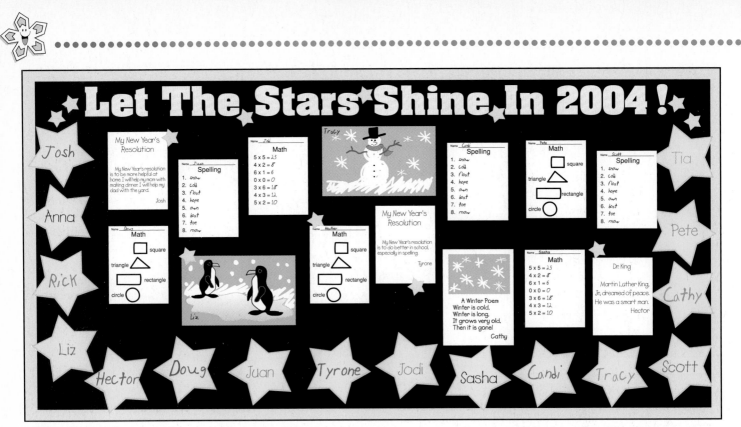

Ring in the new year with this star-studded display. Copy onto construction paper a class supply of the **star patterns** (page 109). Have each student cut out and personalize a star. Cover a bulletin board with black paper; then mount the stars, the title, and a sample of each child's best work. Ask students to replace their work samples weekly. The future definitely looks bright!

Pam Sowatsky—Gr. 3, St. Josaphat School, Saginaw, MI

Display each student's wish for the new year with a lucky penny, and these wishes won't soon be forgotten! Give each child an index card to which you have taped a shiny new penny. Ask the youngsters to write their wishes for the new year on the cards; then mount the cards, along with an enlarged **wishing well pattern** (page 112) as shown. Encourage students to make wishes that would have a positive effect on several people.

Maureen Martin, Northport, NY

The future looks bright at this new year's display. Using the **bear and lightbulb patterns** (page 113), make student copies of the lightbulb pattern and create a large bear cutout like the one shown. Mount the cutout and the title. Have each child label a lightbulb pattern with a new year's wish for the world and then decorate and cut out his bulb. Mount the completed projects for all to see.

Mary F. Williams—Learning Disabilities Tutor, Miamisburg City Schools, Miamisburg, OH

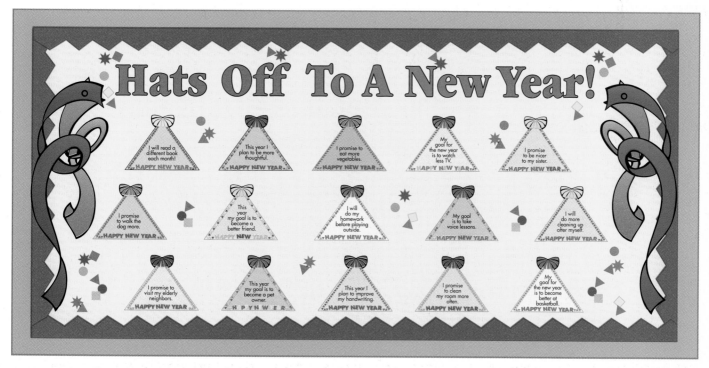

Welcome the new year with a festive display of party hats and confetti! On a construction paper copy of the **hat pattern** (page 114), have each child write a personal goal for the new year. Then have each child cut out and decorate his party hat as desired. Mount the party hats; then enlist your students' help in adding colorful confetti and streamers to the display. Happy New Year!

Ursula O'Donnell—Gr. 2, Meadow Brook School, East Longmeadow, MA

Use this year-round display to promote altruism and foster positive behaviors. Each month showcase a poster or cutout of a person who has contributed to the betterment of others. Add the person's name and a sign that lists his or her most outstanding traits. Then have every student create a personalized cutout for the display. Each time you observe a student or the class exhibiting one of the listed traits, attach a foil star beside that trait. Wow! Look who's making a difference now!

Hope Bertrand—Grs. 2–3, Fremont Elementary School, Bakersfield, CA

In remembrance of Martin Luther King Jr.'s dream of peace and compassion for all, ask students to ponder their dreams for their community. Have each child write his thoughts on white paper and then trim the paper to create one large thought bubble and several small connecting bubbles. Provide the supplies that students need to create self-portraits like the ones shown; then mount each child's project for all to see.

adapted from an idea by Debbie Dalton—Gr. 2, C. M. Bradley Elementary School, Warrenton, VA

Your youngsters will warm right up to this quilt-making project! Remind students that a quilt displayed outside a home signaled to slaves traveling along the Underground Railroad that the home was safe to approach. Then ask each child to design a precut quilt patch for a class freedom quilt. Explain that this quilt will signal to others that your classroom is a safe place for *all* people. Mount the quilt patches and a title patch on a bulletin board covered with colorful paper. Then use a marker to draw stitch lines between the projects.

As students create this display, they learn about famous Black Americans. Each student researches a different Black American hero or heroine and writes several interesting facts about him or her. The student mounts his written work atop a slightly larger piece of construction paper. Then he mounts a picture of the famous person he researched on a heart cutout. (The picture may be cut from a discarded periodical, traced and colored by the student, or student illustrated.) Display the completed projects as shown. Now that's impressive!

Karen Bryant—Gr. 3, Rosa Taylor Elementary School, Macon, GA

A love for literature is in the air! Personalize a **heart pattern** (page 116) for each child and then mount the hearts as shown. Have each child fold a half sheet of paper in half, write on the front the title of a book she absolutely loves, write inside why she loves the book, and then illustrate her work. After each child tells the class about the book she loves, tape her project to her personalized heart. Display the hearts along with an enlarged **bear pattern** (page 115) as shown. Now that's true love!

Sister Maribeth Theis—Gr. 2, Mary of Lourdes Elementary School, Little Falls, MN

The value of love escalates at this two-for-one holiday display! Make a supply of the **heart patterns** (page 116) on red, orange, yellow, green, blue, and purple paper along with a class supply on pink paper. Enlist volunteers to cut out the shapes. Instruct each student to program the pink cutout with his definition of love. Mount the heart cutouts and two black pot cutouts (pattern on page 16) as pictured. Love is definitely in the air!

Helen Hawkins, Beverly Gardens School, Dayton, OH

Showcase a heartwarming collection of student work at this seasonal display. Have each student personalize and decorate a heart-shaped paper topper. After each student has chosen a sample of her best work, mount the work samples, paper toppers, and title as shown. Periodically ask students to replace their displayed work with more current samples. Now that's a true work of "heart"!

Colleen Cori Connally—Gr. 3, Rolling Valley Elementary, Springfield, VA

Your youngsters will be eager to lend a hand in creating this seasonal display! Mount the title; then engage your students in tracing and cutting out their hand shapes from black, white, and red paper. Use the resulting cutouts to form a large heart and arrow. Now that's a "hand-y" heart!

Mary Sue Chatfield—Gr. 1
Central Lee Elementary
Donnellson, IA

Plant a seed of encouragement to create this valentine display that's filled with heartfelt messages. Personalize a large heart card for each student by writing his name and attaching his photo to the card's front. Distribute the cards, making sure that no one receives his own. Inside the card, a student writes a sentence that describes something he especially likes about the person who is pictured. Display the cards as shown.

adapted from an idea by Jeri Daugherity—Gr. 1
Mother Seton School
Emmitsburg, MD

Reel in some valentine fun! To make a construction paper fish, a student cuts a heart shape from each of the following: an eight-inch square (body), a four-inch square (tail), a three-inch square (fin), and a two-inch square (eye). Then he assembles his project and adds desired details with a marker or crayon. Also have each student cut out several heart-shaped air bubbles from his paper scraps. Mount the completed projects as shown.

Kathy Quinlan—Gr. 2, Charles E. Bennett Elementary, Green Cove Springs, FL

This year give your valentine display a clever twist! Ask each student to write a paragraph describing the career she currently finds most appealing. On a white **heart pattern** (page 116), have a student illustrate an adult likeness of herself dressed for the career she chose. Mount the student projects with an enlarged **cupid pattern** (page 117) and a title. The future certainly looks heartwarming!

Diane Fortunato—Gr. 2, Carteret School, Bloomfield, NJ

Get to the heart of the matter with this eye-catching display. Have each student copy and complete the following sentence on a white construction paper **heart pattern** (page 116): "I put my heart into _____ because _____." Using construction paper, crayons or markers, glue, and a variety of other arts-and-crafts supplies (such as lace, glitter, sequins, feathers, and ribbon), students decorate their heart cutouts as desired. Display the hearts along with an enlarged **heart pattern** (page 118) as shown. How sweet it is!

Vickie Genovese, Parkside Elementary, Solon, OH

Spotlight your readers *and* future leaders at this patriotic display. Have each student illustrate herself on drawing paper as a future leader, glue her artwork on red or blue paper, and add foil stars. Display the personalized projects; then staple a laminated poster board strip below each one. A student uses a wipe-off marker to keep her strip programmed with the book title she is currently reading. Read on!

Cynthia Adams—Gr. 3, Jefferson Elementary, Hobbs, NM

Salute your youngsters' presidential dreams at this patriotic display. On an 8" x 10" sheet of white paper, have each child illustrate herself as president of the United States. Then, on a sheet of 8" x 10" writing paper, have each youngster write a story that begins "If I were president...." Mount each student's completed projects on a large sheet of colorful construction paper and display the student work as shown. Now that's impressive!

Linda Hilliard—Grs. 1–3, Arlington, VA

Spring

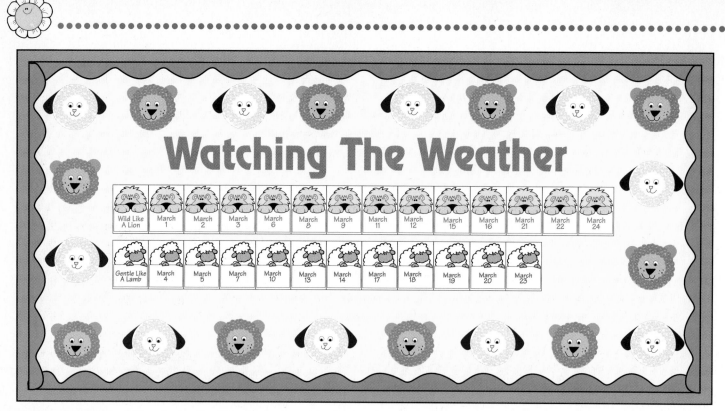

Keeping track of March weather is a breeze at this display. Have each child make a lion or a lamb similar to those shown. Also duplicate and cut out 33 **lion and lamb patterns** (page 120). Program one lion and one lamb card as shown; then mount these two cards, the student projects, and the title. For each day in March, enlist your students' help in categorizing the weather; then date and display the appropriate card.

Peter Tabor—Gr. 1, Weston Elementary, Schofield, WI

Tip your hat to Dr. Seuss in celebration of his birthday—March 2! Give each child a white construction paper copy of the **hat pattern** (page 119) to color. Tell students to leave the second and fourth stripes white. Ask each student to write one word of a rhyming word pair on each white stripe and then cut out the hat. Mount the hats along with a title and an enlarged **cat pattern** (page 119). Happy birthday, Dr. Seuss!

Betsy Crosson—Gr. 1, Pleasant Elementary, Tulare, CA

Turn independent reading into a golden experience! Mount the title and a pot-of-gold cutout as shown. Near the display provide a supply of the **book report pattern** (page 120) and 7" x 10" construction paper rectangles in the colors shown. To make a book report, a child completes a form and cuts it out; then he folds a colored rectangle in half and glues his form inside. Display the completed reports in the shape of a rainbow.

Julie Simpson—Gr. 2, Cherry Elementary, Toledo, OH

A wee bit of writing motivation quickly creates this eye-catching display! Display a writing prompt and an enlarged **leprechaun pattern** (page 121) as shown. Ask each child to write and illustrate a story in response to the prompt. Then exhibit each child's work with a personalized shamrock cutout. And here's a bit of luck for you! Simply update the writing prompt and artwork each month and you have a year-round display.

Tiffany Gosseen—Gr. 1, North Nodaway R-VI Elementary, Hopkins, MO

Ask your budding botanists to give you a hand with this eye-catching display! Mount the background paper and title. Give each small group of students glue, scissors, pencils, a paper stem and flower center, and colorful paper. Demonstrate how to trace a hand on paper to create a leaf, a root, and a petal. Mount each group's completed flower in the class garden and label it as shown.

Patti Ghormley—Gr. 1, Liberty Elementary School, Libertytown, MD

Sprout a renewed interest in class-made books with this springtime display. Precut several paper leaves and stems, make a supply of the **book pattern** (page 122), and mount the title and some paper grass. Each day read aloud a different class-written book and ask a volunteer to create a corresponding flower for the garden. Forgotten titles will be remembered and your students' self-esteem will be in full bloom!

Jennifer Farneski—Gr. 1 Instructional Aide, Berkeley Elementary School, Bloomfield, NJ

Greet the arrival of spring with this picture-perfect vocabulary display! Write a student-generated list of words or phrases that contain the word *spring.* Have each child copy a different word or phrase from the list onto a paper strip; then on desired paper have him write and illustrate a sentence that features this word or phrase. Display the students' work along with the enlarged **spring critter patterns** (page 123) as shown. Spring is everywhere!

Sue Lorey, Arlington Heights, IL

Keep students buzzing with good attendance even when spring fever strikes! Mount a hive cutout and the title as shown. Using construction paper copies of the **bee patterns** (page 124), have each student decorate and cut out a bee. Store the cutouts. Each time 100 percent attendance (or another agreed-upon goal) is achieved, attach a bee cutout to the display. Periodically recognize your youngsters' efforts with a special class privilege.

Tonya Byrd—Gr. 2, William Owen Elementary, Fayetteville, NC

There's no need to ponder how to decorate this display. Just mount the title and a large pond shape—then leave the rest to your students. Using a variety of arts-and-crafts supplies, students can apply their knowledge of pond life to create a pond habitat. Provide several pond-related books for reference. The outcome is a positive learning experience that results in an eye-catching display!

Desiree Palm—Gr. 1, Arrow Springs Elementary, Broken Arrow, OK

Just look what's blooming outside (or is that inside?) your window! Cover a paper-covered bulletin board with clear plastic wrap; then attach windowpanes and a series of shoeboxes—end to end—along the lower edge of the display. Cover the boxes with a student-decorated strip of bulletin-board paper. Fill the resulting window boxes with crumpled brown grocery bags (soil) and student-made flowers attached to green pipe cleaners. Display your students' "sunniest" work in the windows!

Diane Ehrhardt—Gr. 2, Taylor Mills School, Avon, NJ

April Showers Bring...

Are you experiencing April showers when you'd rather be enjoying May flowers? No problem! This student-created display can be in full bloom in no time! Ask each student to draw and color a picture of springtime flowers. Trim and mount the students' artwork as shown; then add paper windowpanes, a paper window shade, and a crepe paper valance. There you have it—a garden of May flowers in April!

adapted from an idea by Linda B. Vaughn—Gr. 2, Franklin Elementary School, Mt. Airy, NC

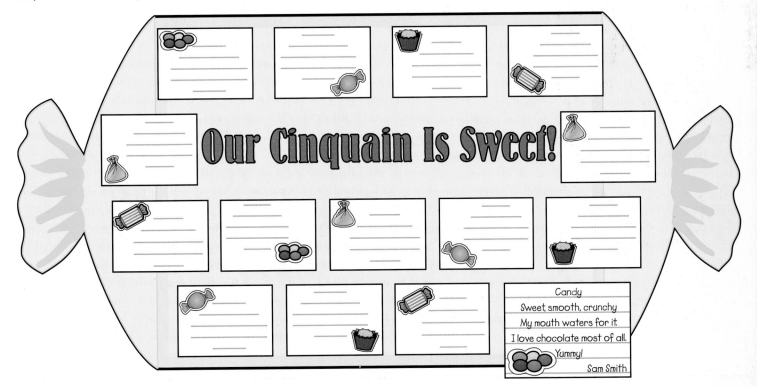

Our Cinquain Is Sweet!

Candy
Sweet, smooth, crunchy
My mouth waters for it.
I love chocolate most of all.
Yummy!
Sam Smith

April, National Poetry Month, is a perfect time to sweeten students' poetry-writing skills! To make the display, attach a paper cutout resembling the end of a wrapped candy to each side of a paper-covered board. Have each child write and publish a candy-related cinquain (or another form of poetry) and showcase the poems as shown. Attach a colorful candy sticker to each one if desired. Now that's a delicious twist!

Tracy Welsch—Gr. 2, Camp Avenue Elementary School, North Merrick, NY

Spill the beans—the jelly beans, that is—about the science process. Mount the title and a large jar cutout that contains a paper **jelly bean pattern** (page 125) labeled for each step of the science process. As students experience the different steps, ask volunteers to post their findings. For added appeal, have each volunteer color-code her work with a jelly bean cutout to show the step on which she is reporting.

Lisa Kelly—Gr. 1, Wood Creek Elementary, Farmington, MI

Showcase your students' "eggs-tra" special artwork at this seasonal display. Mount a large basket cutout and the title. Have each student personalize and decorate a large egg-shaped cutout using paints, markers, or crayons. Display the completed projects as shown. If desired attach construction paper or cellophane grass just inside the basket rim. Now that's a basketful of good eggs!

Sarabeth Sloan—Grs. 3–4 Special Education
Arlington Elementary School #234
Baltimore, MD

Students will be eager to have a crack at this interactive display! Use the **chick and egg patterns** (page 126) to create an equal number of eggs and chicks. Number the eggs and write a review question on each one. Label the chicks with the corresponding answers. Laminate and cut out the patterns; then program the backs of the chicks with numbers for self-checking. A student matches each chick to an egg and then flips the chicks to check his work!

Amy Hall—Substitute Teacher, Robinson, IL

Invite students to lend a hand in preserving the earth! Each student colors and cuts out a copy of the **earth pattern** (page 127). The student also traces one hand atop a sheet of colorful construction paper; then he cuts out and programs the resulting shape with an earth-friendly tip. Mount the hand cutouts around a large globe cutout. Display a snapshot of each child atop his earth cutout. The title says it all—"Earth: It's in Our Hands!"

Mary Jo Kampschnieder—Gr. 2, Howells Community Catholic, Howells, NE

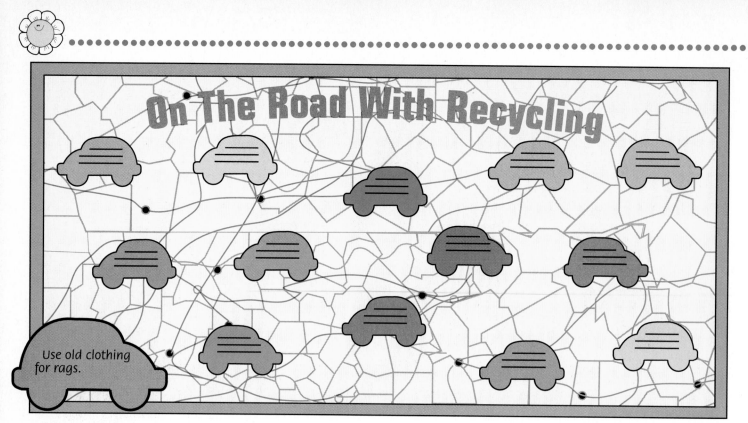

Take a recycling road trip! Cover a display area with discarded road maps and mount the title. Using the **car pattern** (page 127), make a supply of colorful construction paper cars. Each student cuts out a pattern and writes a recycling suggestion on the resulting car shape. Ask each child to share his recycling tip before you mount his cutout on the display. Vroooom!

Gina Parisi—Gr. 2, Demarest School, Bloomfield, NJ

This May encourage students to set their sights on whatever their hearts desire with this unique display. On a large square of colorful paper, have each student complete the sentence, "One day, just MAYbe...." Have students trim their papers to resemble flower blossoms. Mount the blossoms atop crepe paper stems and leaves to create a spectacular flower garden!

Debbie Wiggins, North Myrtle Beach Primary, North Myrtle Beach, SC

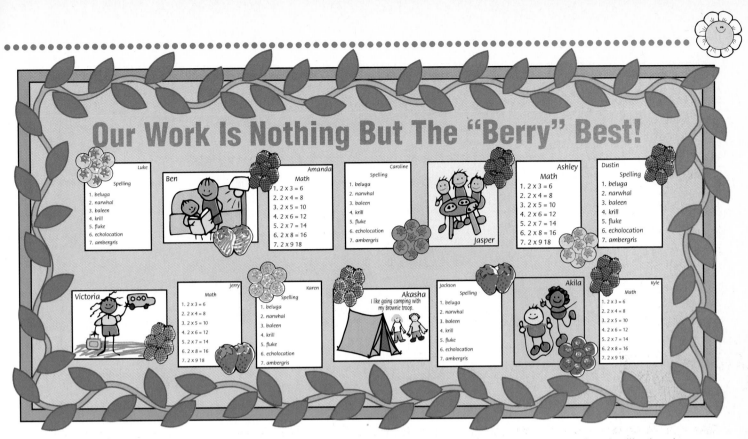

Showcase your students' "berry" best work at this delicious-looking display! Mount the title and a vinelike border. To make a paper topper, a student uses watercolors to paint a **berry pattern** (page 128). When the paint is dry, he cuts out the pattern, spreads a thin layer of glue over it, and sprinkles the glue with clear glitter. Exhibit the student's berry project and a sample of his best work at the display. Dazzling!

Sarah Mertz, Owenton, KY

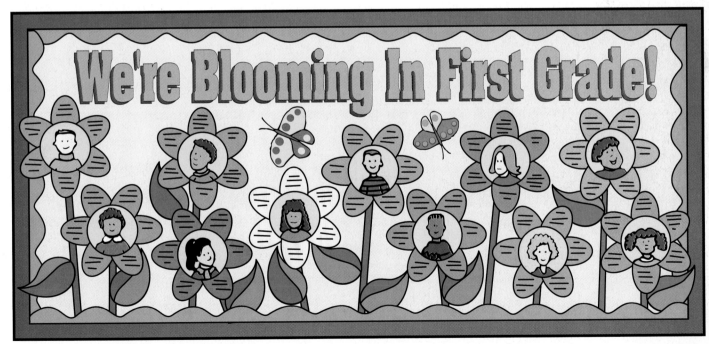

To sow this garden of success, have each student label the petals of a paper flower with things he has learned during the school year and then illustrate himself in the flower's center. As the school year draws to a close, ask one student per day to pick his flower and share it with his classmates. On the last day of school you'll have very proud youngsters and a nearly empty display!

Lynn White—Gr. 1, Ellisville Elementary, Ellisville, MO

A Picture-Perfect Year!

Picture this—an end-of-the-year display that's quick and easy to put up and take down! Display an enlarged **camera pattern** (page 129), the title, and a collection of mounted snapshots that reflect a variety of events from the past school year. Use the completed display as a prompt for end-of-the-year student discussions and writing activities. Students who may be in your room next year will also enjoy taking a peek at the pictures.

Patricia Smith, Jackman School, Toledo, OH

After you've featured every child on your "Star Of The Week" display, transform it into an end-of-the-year reading motivator. Change the heading, attach two labeled envelopes as shown, and tuck a supply of **star patterns** (page 109) in each envelope. When a student reads a book, she writes her name and the book's title on the desired star and pins it to the display. Each day select a few posted stars and let these readers shine!

Kristin A. McLaughlin—Gr. 1, Daniel Boone Area Elementary, Boyertown, PA

Give your end-of-the-year display a space-age spin! Cover a bulletin board with black paper, accent it with foil stars, and add the title. Have each child describe a highlight from the past school year on a colorful **comet pattern** (page 130), then cut it out. Next he uses a toilet-tissue roll and assorted other supplies to design a rocket. Mount the projects and you have an out-of-this-world finale to the school year!

Mary Mahaffey—Gr. 3, Harrisburg Academy, Wormleysburg, PA

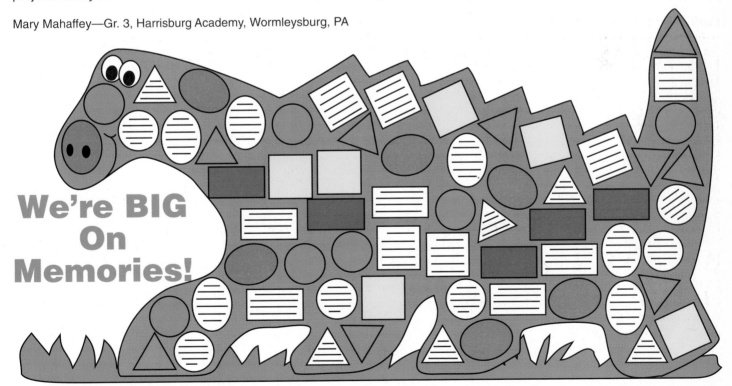

Make a big impression with this colossal collection of memories. A student traces a shape template (oval, square, etc.) onto writing paper and art paper. He cuts out each shape; then, on the lined cutout, he describes a favorite memory from the school year. Assist students in arranging the cutouts on colorful paper to resemble a dinosaur; then have them glue the cutouts in place. Cut out the dinosaur shape and embellish it as desired. Mount the one-of-a-kind lizard for all to enjoy!

adapted from an idea by Sharma Houston—Gr. 2, Pearsontown Elementary, Durham, NC

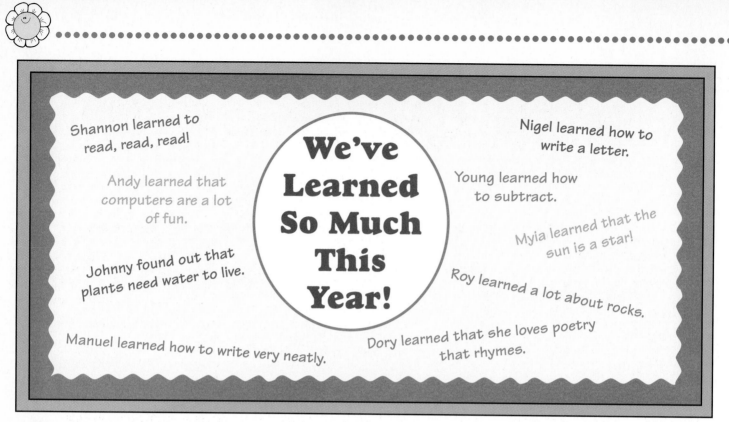

This end-of-the-year bulletin board is really smart! Mount the title on a recycled backdrop. Ask each child to tell one thing she learned during the past school year and use a colorful marker to write her comment on the paper. Students will be proud of their accomplishments, and you'll have a colorful display that's easy to remove on the final day of school.

Kari Mart—Gr. 1, LaMoure School, LaMoure, ND

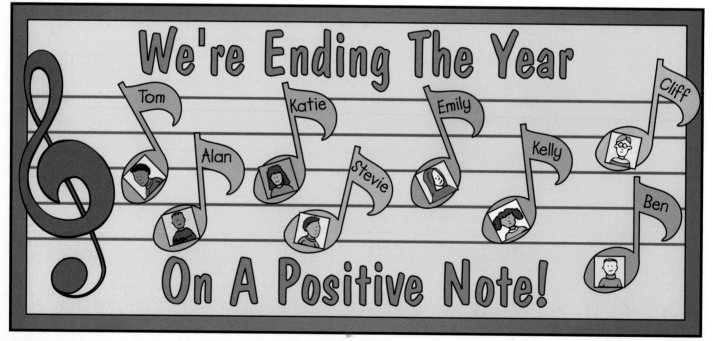

Make musical memories with this end-of-the-year display. Mount a **note pattern** (page 131) for each student. If student photos are not available, ask each child to illustrate herself on precut paper; then attach the students' artwork to their personalized music notes. Each day spotlight a different student and write a note from the class for the student that includes fond memories about her from throughout the school year.

Lynn White—Gr. 1, Ellisville Elementary, Ellisville, MO

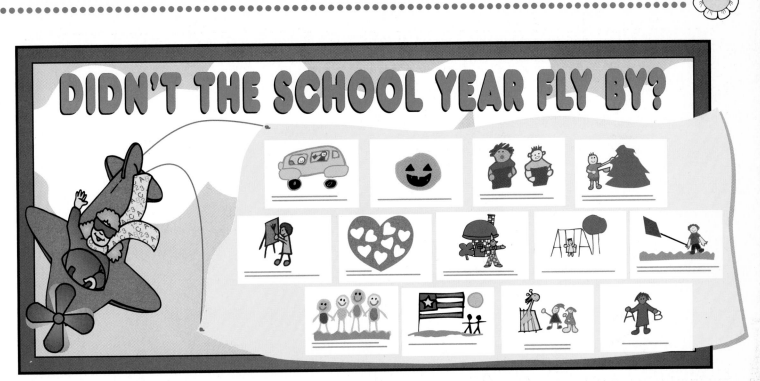

The sky's the limit! Ask each child to illustrate and write a brief description about a different event from the past school year. As a class activity, sequence the student-illustrated events; then mount their artwork on a high-flying banner attached to an enlarged **airplane pattern** (page 132) like the one shown. Wow! The school year really did fly by!

Mary Mahaffey—Gr. 3, The Harrisburg Academy, Wormleysburg, PA

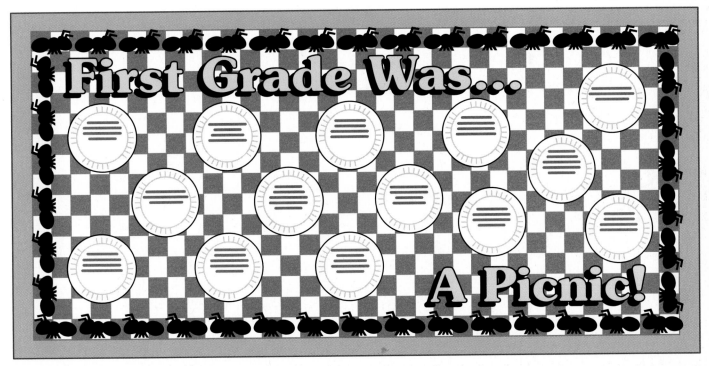

Here's an end-of-the-year display that's sure to create quite a stir! Have each student personalize and program a thin white paper plate with a favorite memory from the past school year. Mount the plates on a checkered backdrop. Add the title and a border of student-designed ants. Now that's a picnic!

Holly L. Davis—Gr. 1, Rural Retreat Elementary, Rural Retreat, VA

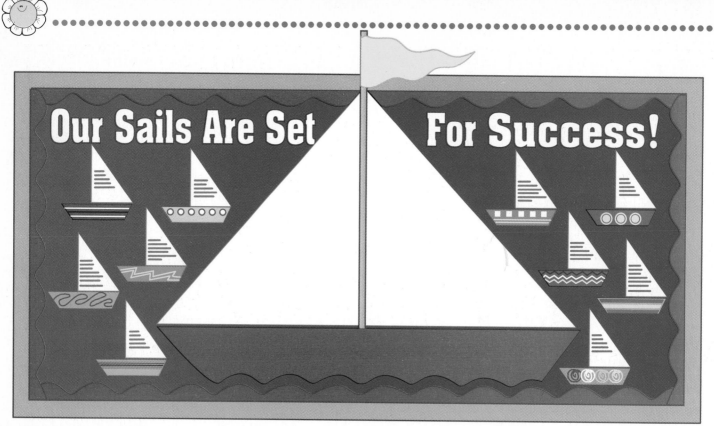

Making this end-of-the-year display is a breeze! Cover a bulletin board with an ocean of blue paper and mount a large sailboat cutout and a title. Give each child a copy of the **sailboat pattern** (page 133). Have each youngster cut out the pattern and personalize the hull. Then have each student write his goal(s) for next year on the sail. Display each child's sailboat as shown. Smooth sailing!

Camilla Law—Gr. 3, St. Timothy's School, Raleigh, NC

Keep the entire class on course by putting each student in the driver's seat! A child adds his name and likeness to a **car pattern** (page 135); then he colors the pattern and cuts it out. Next, he writes (on a precut construction paper shape) one thing he expects to learn in school the following year. Display the projects as shown. Vroom!

Trina Taylor—Gr. 2, High Point Elementary, Cedar Hill, TX

To create this crowd-pleasing display, ask students to brainstorm their favorite events from the past school year. List their ideas on the chalkboard. Then, on precut story paper, have each child illustrate and describe a different event from the list. Showcase each student's work on a construction paper circle along with an enlarged **seal pattern** (page 134) as shown. Now that's a class act!

Darlene Weir—Gr. 2, South Elementary School, Mt. Carmel, IL

Students will like lending a hand with this sunny summer send-off. Mount a large sun cutout that sports student-made hand-shaped rays. Ask each child to write a prediction about the upcoming summer on a sheet of white paper, then trim his paper to create a cloud shape. Post the predictions on the display. What a warm welcome to summertime!

Denise Tinucci Farrell—Gr. 3, St. Joseph School, Collingdale, PA

Splish, splash, summer's almost here! For this display a child describes on paper an activity she hopes to enjoy this summer. She trims her paper into a speech bubble. Then she colors a copy of the **inner tube pattern** (page 135) and cuts it out. Next, she uses art supplies to fashion a likeness of herself from her waist up and glues it to the inner tube as shown. Showcase each child's projects together.

Catherine Broome—Gr. 1, Melbourne, FL

Summer dreams turn into summertime snapshots with a little help from your students. Follow up a discussion of your students' summer plans by having each child illustrate himself engaged in an activity he hopes to enjoy this summer. Mount the resulting snapshots along with an enlarged **photographer pattern** (page 136) as shown. Have each student glue a small, black triangle in each corner of his artwork. Smile for the camera!

adapted from an idea by Theodora Gallagher—Gr. 1, Carteret School, Bloomfield, NJ

Anytime

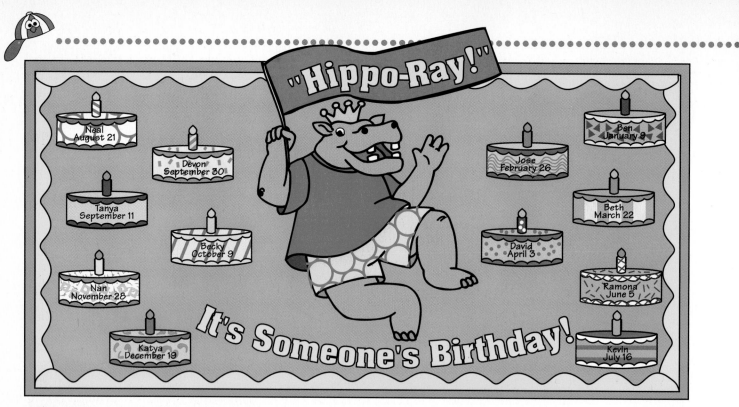

Recognize your youngsters' birthdays in a big way with this year-round display! Mount the title and a large birthday character like the one shown. Write each child's name and birthday on a white construction paper copy of the **cake pattern** (page 137). Then have each child decorate and cut out his birthday cake. Mount the completed cutouts onto the display. Plan to recognize every student's birthday during the school year—even those that occur during the summer months.

Diane Fortunato—Gr. 2, Carteret School, Bloomfield, NJ

Students work as a team to piece together this display. On bulletin board paper cut to the desired size and shape, draw one interlocking puzzle piece per student. Mark the lower edge of each piece with a dot; then cut apart and distribute the pieces. Each child personalizes his puzzle piece to reflect his special interests. After students have shared their puzzle pieces with their classmates, they work together to reassemble the puzzle. Display the completed project for all to see. Now that's a perfect fit!

Diana Vrooman—Gr. 3, College Station, TX

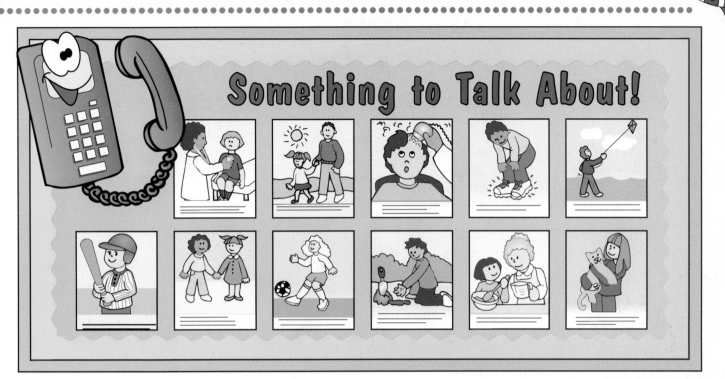

Something to Talk About!

Spotlight your youngsters' weekend experiences at this eye-catching display. Each Monday, every child who has a weekend experience that she'd like to share with the class creates an illustration and a caption about it. Showcase these projects along with an enlarged **phone pattern** (page 137). Set aside time for each child to explain her work and provide added details about the pictured event.

Donna L. Hall—Grs. 1–2, Fairview Elementary, St. Louis, MO

This year-round bulletin board is sure to steal the scene! Near the end of each week, select one student to illustrate his favorite event from that week. To make a clapboard, the student glues one end of a 1½" x 12" white construction paper strip to the corner of a 9" x 12" sheet of white construction paper as shown. Then he illustrates his scene, writes a related caption below his artwork, and designs a border for his clapboard. Display the completed works with the enlarged **light** and **character patterns** (page 138) as shown.

adapted from an idea by Diane Fortunato—Gr. 2, Carteret School, Bloomfield, NJ

Applaud the efforts and contributions of a student teacher, parent helper(s), a school principal, a librarian, or other select individuals with this handy display. Mount a desired title. Have each child trace one of his hands on colorful construction paper and then cut out, personalize, and program the resulting shape with an appropriate note of thanks. Mount the cutouts. If desired, spotlight a different person each week.

Phil Forsythe—Gr. 3, Northeastern Elementary School, Bellefontaine, OH

There's no monkey business here, just plenty of tasteful suggestions! As students munch on potato chips, lead them in brainstorming ideas for classroom cooperation. Then each child folds a yellow paper rectangle in half and trims away the corners. He writes his name and adds desired potato chip details on the front; then inside he writes his plans for chipping in and cooperating. Mount the projects along with the enlarged **monkey patterns** (page 139) as shown. Bet ya can't read just one!

Alice Gershon, Kildeer Countryside School, Long Grove, IL

Look Who Has Been Caught Being Kind!

There's no catch limit at this fishy display! Mount the title and a fishnet; then use the **fish patterns** (page 140) to create a supply of colorful fish. Store the fish patterns, pencils, crayons, and scissors near the display. When a child observes or experiences an act of kindness, he describes the event on a fish pattern. Next, he customizes, cuts out, and displays the fish for all to see. Wow! What a catch!

Debbie Sietsema—Gr. 2, Allendale Public School, Allendale, MI

Always "Bee" a Friend!

1. be kind
2. be fair
3. be polite
4. be honest
5. be helpful
6. be thoughtful
7. be a good listener
8. be willing to share

Foster friendship with this honey of a display! Write a student-generated list of friendship tips on a large hive cutout. Have each child personalize and color a **bee pattern** (page 140) and then cut it out. Mount the title, hive, and cutouts. To keep students abuzz with friendship, occasionally read aloud tips from the list and ask students who practice them to buzz! Reward exemplary acts of friendship with bite-size Bit•O•Honey candy bars.

Jennifer Balogh-Joiner—Gr. 2, Franklin Elementary, Franklin, NJ

Keep your happy hive humming with this easy-to-manage helper display. Mount a beehive like the one shown and several sets of bee wings that you have labeled with desired job descriptions. Have each student personalize and cut out a **bee pattern** (page 141). Pin a bee cutout to each pair of wings; then store the remaining bees in the hive. Each week, assign new jobs using an established method of rotation.

Tara Livingston—Special Education, Valley Park School, Overland Park, KS

Get to the point with this easy-to-make helper display! Label a **pencil pattern** (page 142) with each desired job description and label one "Off Duty." Mount the cutouts and title on a newspaper-covered bulletin board. Attach a press-on pocket containing individual student snapshots beside the "Off Duty" pencil; then pin one snapshot from the pocket beside each pencil. Assign weekly jobs using an established method of rotation.

Joan Frickleton—Grs. 2–4, Glen Oak Continuous Progress School, Peoria, IL

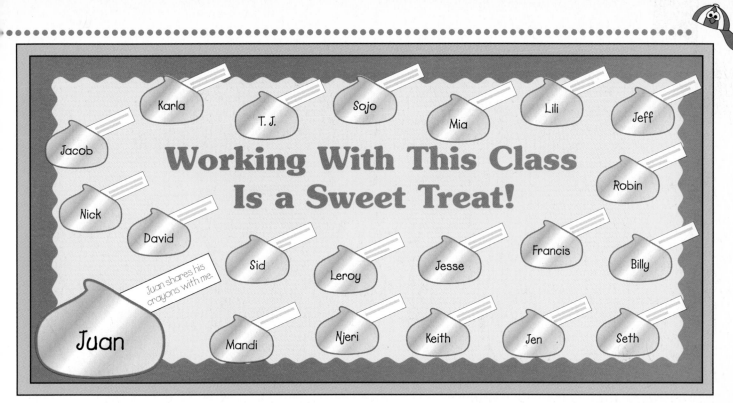

Give students' self-esteem a sweet boost! Have each child write on a paper strip a compliment about a different classmate. Tape each strip to a foil-wrapped **candy kiss pattern** (page 143) personalized for that child. Display the projects as shown. Each week ask students to submit compliments for different classmates, and then use them to update the display.

Jill Hamilton—Gr. 1, Schoeneck Elementary, Stevens, PA

Propel your students' self-esteem to extraordinary heights with this star-studded display. Have each child write his name in the center of a large **star pattern** (page 109) and then illustrate one of his special talents, hobbies, or favorite things in each star point. Provide time for each child to explain his star to his classmates; then display the projects as shown. There's no doubt about it—everyone's a star!

Kathie Eckelkamp—Gr. 2, Most Precious Blood School, St. Louis, MO

Spotlight budding authors at this 3-D display! Use wallpaper, fabric, and other decorative items to fashion a chair, a lamp, and a table. Also create laminated posters for showcasing author information. Each week draw an outline of the featured author on paper and cut it out. The student decorates the cutout to resemble himself and designs a book cover. Display these items and use a wipe-off marker to program the posters with information about the author. Exhibit some of the author's original work nearby. Autographs, anyone?

Sarah Mertz—Grs. 1–2, Owenton, KY

Lasso your wranglers' outstanding work at this star-studded display. Mount an enlarged **cowboy character pattern** (page 144) and title. Have each youngster create a personalized badge cutout, as shown, and then round up a sample of his finest work. Display each work sample with its corresponding badge. To keep the display current, invite wranglers to replace their work as frequently as desired. Yee-hah!

Kathy Marquar—Gr. 1, J. E. Moss Elementary, Antioch, TN

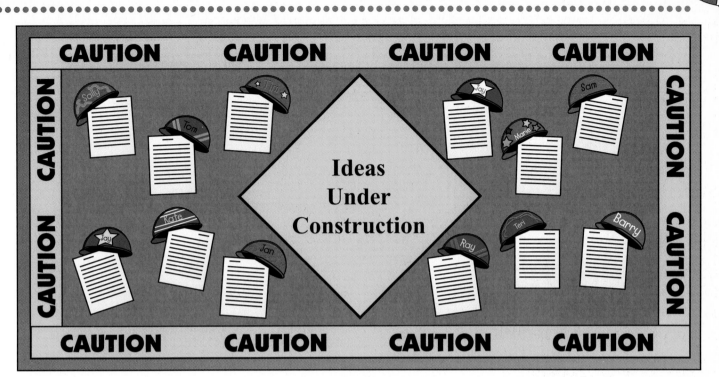

Look who's hard at work! Mount the title and a border of yellow caution tape. Then have each student personalize and cut out a construction paper copy of the **hard-hat pattern** (page 145). Laminate the cutouts and slit the dotted lines. Ask each student to choose a sample of her best work; then display the papers with their matching cutouts. Invite students to replace their work samples as frequently as desired.

adapted from an idea by VaReane Gray Heese, Omaha, NE

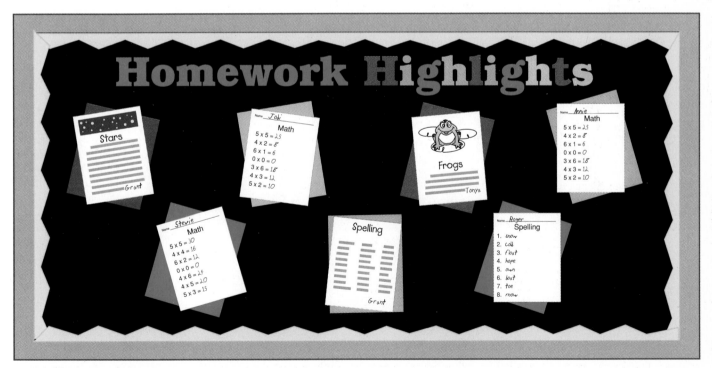

This colorful display is sure to create enthusiasm for homework. Use assorted colors of neon paper to create the title and the individual backdrops for students' homework. When a student's homework merits extra recognition, attach his paper to the display. Keep the display fresh by frequently replacing the posted homework papers with more current samples.

Judy Chunn—Grs. 2–3, Westminster School, Nashville, TN

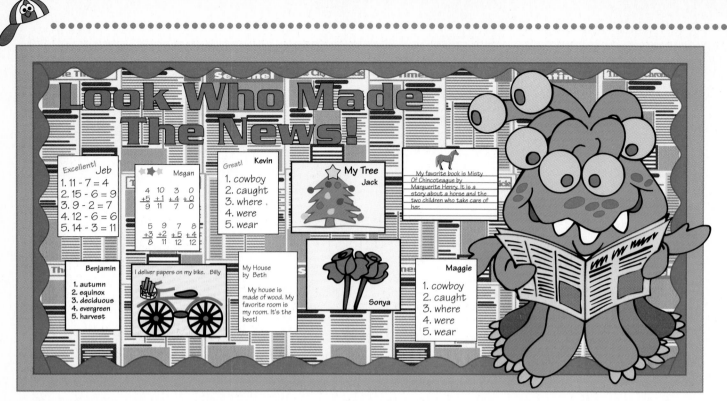

Spread classroom news at this easy-to-make display! Cover a bulletin board with newspaper; then add the title, a border, and an enlarged **monster pattern** (page 146). Showcase a perpetual assortment of outstanding student papers, classroom awards, and other noteworthy news for all to see!

Jeanine Fanto-Healy—Gr. 2, Manor Heights Elementary, Casper, WY

Showcase your youngsters' finest work on this eye-catching display. Mount the title; then have each student personalize and cut out a construction paper copy of the **pencil pattern** (page 142). Laminate the pencil cutouts for durability. Ask each student to choose a current sample of his best work; then display each work sample with its corresponding cutout. To keep the display up-to-date, encourage students to replace their work samples as frequently as desired.

Annette Rupert—Gr. 2, Colorado Christian School, Denver, CO

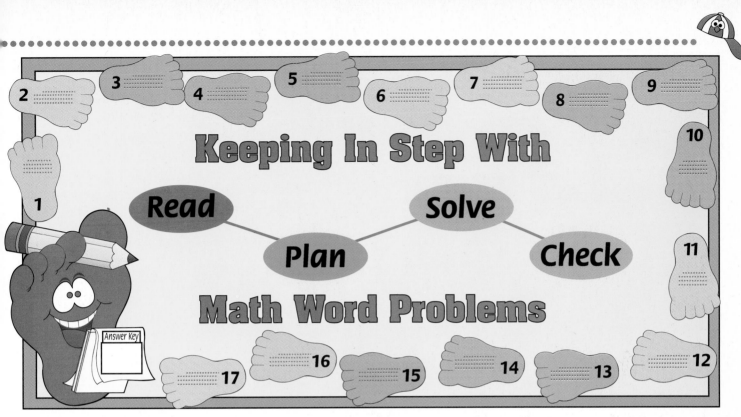

Take the fancy footwork out of solving word problems! Mount the title, an enlarged **foot character pattern** (page 147), and the four steps to solving a word problem. To create the border, have each child write a math word problem on a numbered **footprint pattern** (page 147); then mount the pattern as shown. Challenge students to use the four-step method to solve the word problems their classmates created. Provide an answer key at the display if desired.

Gina Parisi—Basic Skills Grs. 1–6, Brookdale School, Bloomfield, NJ

Provide a year's worth of estimation practice at this fetching display! Have each student personalize and cut out a **bone pattern** (page 148). Mount the cutouts, the title, and a canine character. Each Monday attach a bag of items to be estimated and blank adding-machine tape for student answers. A student writes his estimate next to his personalized cutout. He may adjust his estimate throughout the week. On Friday divide the contents of the bag among your students for an official count.

Maryann D'Amelio—Gr. 2
Roy Gomm Elementary School
Reno, NV

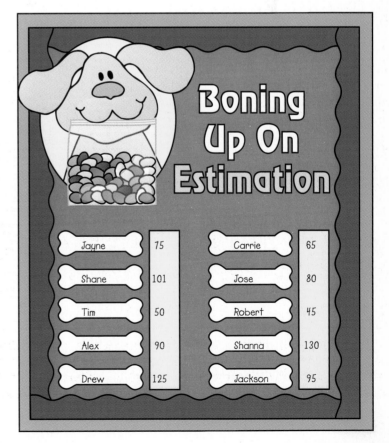

Rub-a-dub-dub! This interactive display may cause student interest in math to bubble over! Enlarge and color the **bear pattern** (page 149). Program one side of several bubble cutouts with math-related problems. Use pushpins to display the bubbles facedown. When time allows, choose a bubble and challenge students to solve its corresponding problem. When the problem is solved, reattach the bubble to the display faceup. Be sure to plan a bubble-related celebration when all the problems are solved!

Amy Barsanti—Gr. 2, Pines Elementary School, Plymouth, NC

You'll have bumper-to-bumper traffic at this interactive display! A child draws a driver and one or more passengers on a tagboard **car pattern** (page 150) and then colors the pattern and cuts it out. Label white rectangles with math facts— one per car. Program the back of each resulting license plate for self-checking. Use Velcro fasteners to secure each plate to a car. Keep students interested in maneuvering the math facts by periodically switching the plates or providing new ones.

Sarah Mertz, Owenton, KY

Measurement skills live happily ever after at this interactive display! Mount the title, a tower cutout, a likeness of Rapunzel, and a laminated growth chart. Use yellow yarn and tape to make five hair extensions of varying lengths. Display one extension on Monday and secure a hair bow at the top; then add one extension per day. Every day students measure carefully to find out how much Rapunzel's hair has grown. Conclude each day by writing on the growth chart (with wipe-off marker) a class-provided measurement. Next, have the students refer to the information on the chart to answer measurement-related questions. To repeat the weeklong activity, wipe off the chart. Then remove the hair extensions and return them to the display in a different order.

Spring Bailey—Gr. 2
Frances Mack Elementary School
Gaston, SC

Measuring Rapunzel's Hair

Growth Chart

Monday	=	10 inches
Tuesday	=	16 inches
Wednesday	=	_____
Thursday	=	_____
Friday	=	_____

Our Smiles Really Measure Up!

30 inches = 2 1/2 feet

Student smiles really add up at this math-related display! Working in pairs, each child uses a different piece of red yarn to measure the width of his partner's smile; then he trims the yarn to smile width and presents it to his partner. Next, each child uses a ruler to measure his yarn. Total these measurements; then have each child make a self-portrait sporting his red-yarn smile! Display as shown. Cheese!

Cathy T. Howlett—Gr. 3, Franklin Elementary, Mt. Airy, NC

Alphabetizing practice is a breeze at this hands-on display! Securely attach three lengths of heavy string or plastic clothesline to a bulletin board; then clip 26 clothespins to the lines. Copy 26 **T-shirt patterns** (page 151) onto tagboard and program each with a different alphabet letter. Instruct each student to decorate a pattern with pictures of items that begin with that letter's sound. Laminate these projects for durability; then store them in a laundry basket. Each morning ask a different student to clip the T-shirt cutouts to the line in alphabetical order. Remove the cutouts at the end of each day.

Julie Erthal—Gr. 1, Thomas Jefferson School, Alton, IL

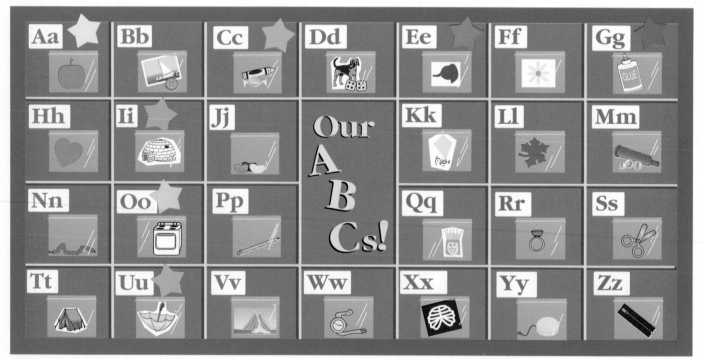

Beginning sounds are in the bag! Use yarn to visually divide a bulletin board; then add the title. In each remaining section secure an alphabet card, a star (if the letter makes more than one initial sound), and an empty resealable plastic bag. Invite students to place paper cutouts and small nonperishable items in the bags to represent the beginning sounds. Now that's a hands-on display with year-round appeal!

Linda Parris—Gr. 1, West Hills Elementary, Knoxville, TN

Propel spelling skills to extraordinary heights all year long! Cover tagboard stars with foil; then attach a laminated card to each star. Mount the stars, the title, an enlarged **rocket pattern** (page 152), and a trail of holiday lights. Every week use a wipe-off marker to program the cards with spelling words. Wipe the cards clean before test time. Each child who aces the test adds a star sticker to the display. Illuminate the lights for added spelling inspiration!

Rebecca Kielas—Grs. 1–2, Badger State Baptist School, Milwaukee, WI

You can count on this easy-to-create display being a HUGE hit with your students. To create a booklet holder for each child, staple the sides and lower edge of a one-foot strip of green corrugated bulletin board border to the display. Each student slips his completed dinosaur story into a holder. The "dino-mite" tales are now "dino-mite" reading selections! (For a seasonal display, feature bunny-shaped books with the title "Hop to It!")

Kathy Quinlan—Gr. 2, Charles E. Bennett Elementary, Green Cove Springs, FL

Invite budding poets to go out on a limb and publish their prose under "The Poet Tree." Mount a tree-shaped cutout, the title, and a few paper leaves labeled with the names of poets your students will recognize. When a student is ready to showcase an original poem at the display, attach a leaf bearing her name to the tree. Encourage students to periodically replace their poems with more current samples.

Karen Dubé Lamas—Grs. 1–5 Gifted, Campbell Drive Elementary, Miami, FL

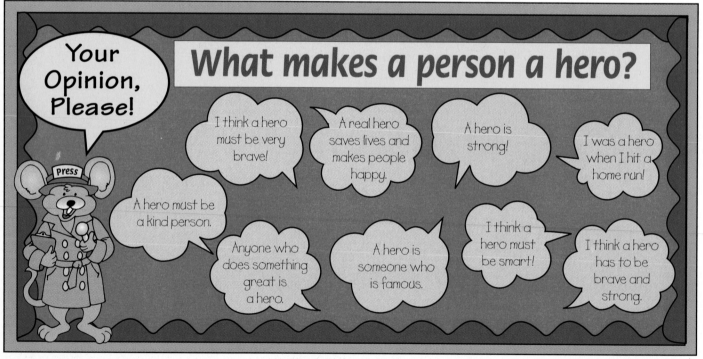

Students will be eager to share their written opinions at this easy-to-create display. Mount an enlarged **mouse reporter pattern** (page 153), a title, and a laminated tagboard strip. Each week use a wipe-off marker to program the laminated strip with a different opinion-seeking question. A student pens her opinion on provided paper, trims her paper to resemble a speech bubble, and then showcases her work at the display.

Cindy Fingerlin—Gr. 3, Eisenhower School, Parlin, NJ

72

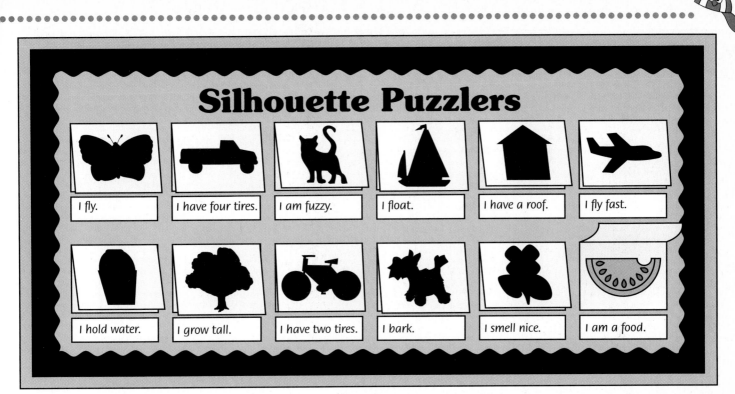

Silhouette Puzzlers

I fly.	
I have four tires.	
I am fuzzy.	
I float.	
I have a roof.	
I fly fast.	
I hold water.	
I grow tall.	
I have two tires.	
I bark.	
I smell nice.	
I am a food.	

Prompt plenty of creative thinking with shapely silhouettes! Each child cuts a different object from a discarded magazine, traces the cutout on black paper, cuts along the resulting outline, and glues her cutouts on folded construction paper as shown. Then she writes a silhouette-related clue on provided paper. The resulting interactive display will be buzzing with creative thoughts!

Jill Hamilton—Gr. 1, Schoeneck Elementary, Stevens, PA

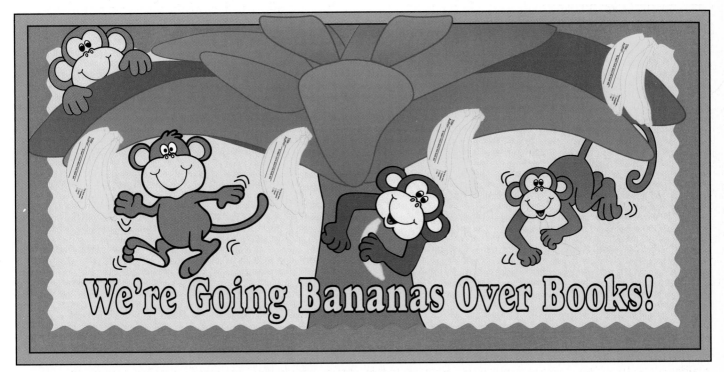

This motivational reading display will have students going bananas over books! Mount a large three-dimensional treetop, an enlarged **monkey pattern** or two (page 154), and the title. Using the **banana pattern** (page 154), make a supply of banana-shaped book reports. Each time a child reads a book, he completes and cuts out a banana report. Display the bananas in bunches. Encourage students to check out their classmates' "a-peel-ing" reading recommendations!

Katherine V. Gartner—Grs. 1–2 Special Education, Oxhead Road Elementary School, Centereach, NY

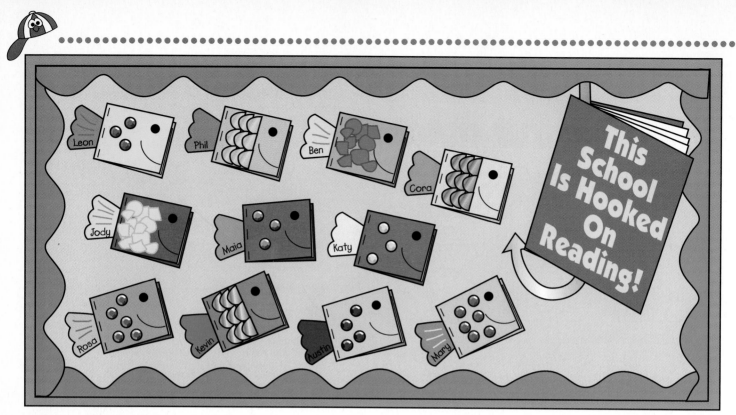

Make a splash with this school of student-made booklets! To make a booklet, trim a 3" x 4" paper rectangle to resemble a fish tail. Next, staple one end of the tail and a supply of blank paper between two 4½" x 6" construction paper covers. Each child personalizes and decorates his booklet cover; then he lists and describes his favorite books inside. Showcase the projects as shown. What a catch!

Sharma Houston—Gr. 2, Pearsontown Elementary, Durham, NC

Promote independent reading with this "bone-afide" plan! Trim the top four inches from a class supply of paper lunch bags. Each child writes his name and colors pawprints on a bag. Mount the bags, an enlarged **canine character pattern** (page 155), and the title. For each book a child reads, he completes a **book review bone pattern** (page 155), cuts it out, and stores it in his bag. You can see who's reading what, and the students can sniff out their classmates' favorite books. "Paws-itively" perfect!

Kimberly Hawk—Gr. 3, March School, Easton, PA

Create a stir with this cool 3-D reading display! For every child, cover an empty tissue box with white paper. On each of three sides of his resulting ice cube, a student writes the title of a favorite book and illustrates a scene from it. Mount the projects as shown. Now that's a refreshing way for youngsters to share their favorite literature!

Julia Brown—Gr. 3
Forest City Elementary
Forest City, NC

Take reading interest to new heights with a garden of student-made reading recommendations. To recommend a book, a student completes and cuts out a yellow copy of the **flower patterns** (page 156). He puts a drop of glue at each • and attaches a programmed petal. At the ▲, he glues a 4½-inch brown circle. He then glues a long, green stem bearing leaf cutouts to the back of the flower. Display the projects as shown. When a child is intrigued by a classmate's recommendation, he carefully plucks a programmed petal from the sunflower and stores it until his next trip to the library.

Tonya Byrd—Gr. 2, William H. Owen Elementary, Hope Mills, NC

Getting the word out about your students' favorite storybook characters is a foolproof plan for promoting an interest in reading. A child illustrates his favorite character on a white oval and then he names and describes the character on a second white oval of the same size. He glues these cutouts to opposite sides of a slightly larger brown oval. Use a hole puncher and ribbon length to display each project. Read on!

Pam Wilson—Gr. 3, Ebenezer School, Statesville, NC

Make a fashion statement and motivate your young readers with this book-and-blue-jeans display! Poke a paperback in each back pocket of a pair of jeans; then secure the jeans to the display. Using the **pocket patterns** (page 157), make a supply of book report forms on light blue construction paper. To make a book report, a child writes his name, the date, the book's title and author, and a description of the book. Then he cuts out and decorates the resulting pocket as desired.

Janet O'Bleness—Grs. 1–4, Wells–Carey Elementary, Keokuk, IA

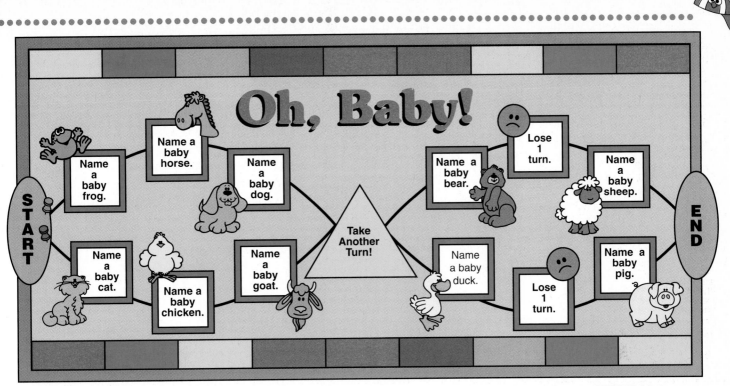

Review any topic with this interactive display! Create a gameboard; then insert two pushpins at START. Make a die that has values of "1" and "2." To play, one of two students (or teams) picks a pathway, rolls the die, and moves his pushpin. If he correctly follows the direction, he stays there. An incorrect response at any point along the game-board returns the player to START. The first player to reach END wins. Frequently change the programming to keep student interest high.

Terrie Guest Yang—Grs. K–1, Hsin-chu International School, Hsin-chu, Taiwan

This year-round display is great for reinforcing geography skills. Ask students to bring to school postcards showing different places in the United States. Have each student who brings a postcard tell something about the site on his card. Then display his card and use a yarn length to show its location on an enlarged **map pattern** (page 81). Invite students to continue bringing postcards to school throughout the year. Geography has never been more fun!

Alesia M. Richards—Grs. 1–2, Apple Pie Ridge Elementary School, Winchester, PA

For this neighborly display, students work independently to create paper lunch bag dwellings and then pool their projects to create a neighborhood. To make a dwelling, partially fill a lunch bag with crumpled newspaper; then fold down and staple the top of the bag closed before decorating the dwelling as desired. Use the same technique to create a schoolhouse from a large-size paper bag that has been spray-painted red. Name the neighborhood for your school principal and use teachers' names for streets. For added fun, cut the border from a discarded road map.

Emily Navidad—Art Educator, Morganton Road Elementary School, Fayetteville, NC

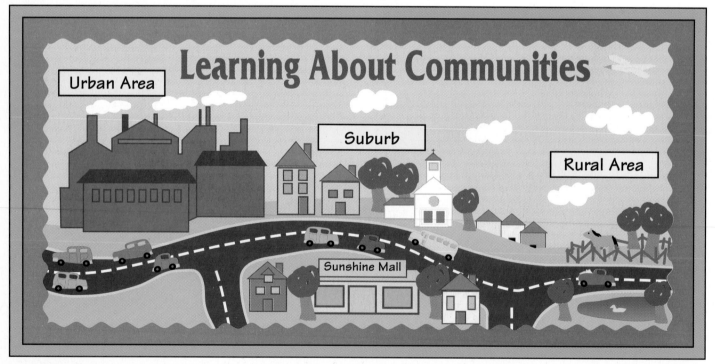

Culminate your community study with this student-made display. Have your students craft the construction paper components (buildings, homes, cars, scenery, etc.) that are needed to represent an urban area, a suburb, and a rural area. Mount the cutouts onto a background like the one shown; then label the three resulting communities. There you have it—a picture-perfect review of communities!

Joyce G. Burnette—Gr. 3, Southwest Elementary School, Winston-Salem, NC

Bring the community into focus at this informative display! Each child writes a brief report about a community landmark and mounts it on construction paper. Then she folds her project in half (keeping the writing inside), tapes a snapshot of the location on the front, and glues a **camera pattern** (page 158) over the photo so that the landmark is seen through the lens opening. Mount the picture-perfect projects along with an enlarged **camera character pattern** (page 158) as shown.

Kathleen Cowin—Gr. 2, Munson Primary School, Mulvane, KS

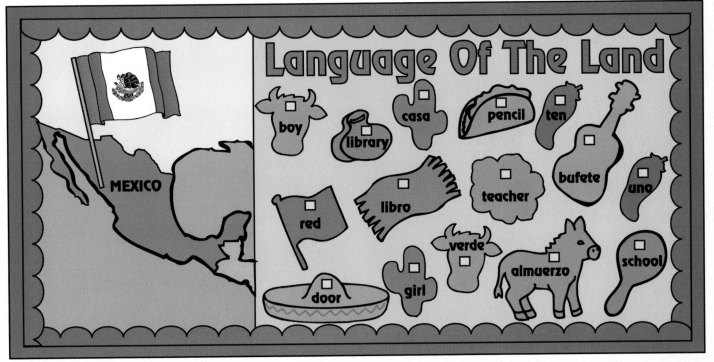

Whether your social studies excursion takes you to Mexico or Italy, don't leave home without this manipulative display! Mount the title and a cutout of the country; then have each student create a cutout that represents the country. On each student's cutout, write a different foreign word or phrase; then program the backs of the cutouts with the corresponding English meanings. Attach a loop side piece of Velcro fastener to each side of the cutouts; then use hook side pieces of Velcro fastener to attach the cutouts to the display. Students are sure to enjoy learning the language of the land!

Gina Bracciale—Substitute Teacher, Miami Country Day School, Miami Shores, FL

Pattern
Use with "Vacation Time" on page 4 and
"Oh, the Places We Can Go!" on page 77.

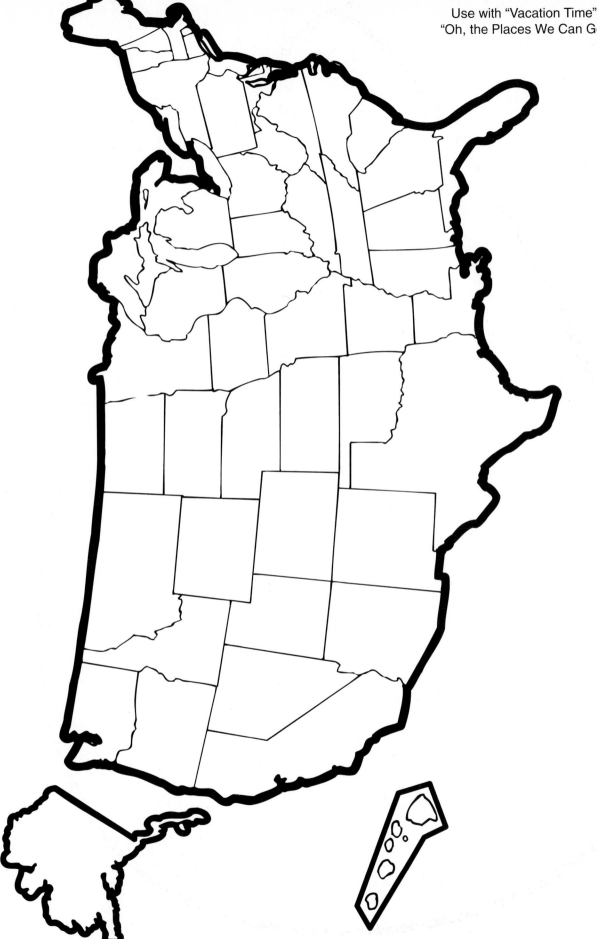

Pattern

Use with "Our Family Trees" on page 6.

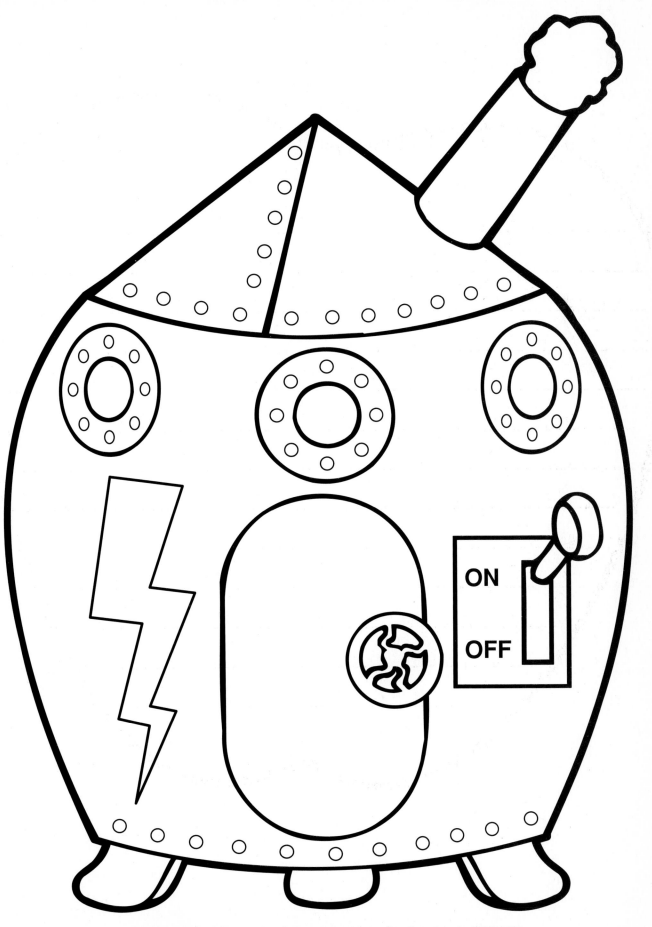

Pattern

Use with "We've Been on the Move!" on page 7.

Use with "We Are the Key to a Great Year!" on page 8.

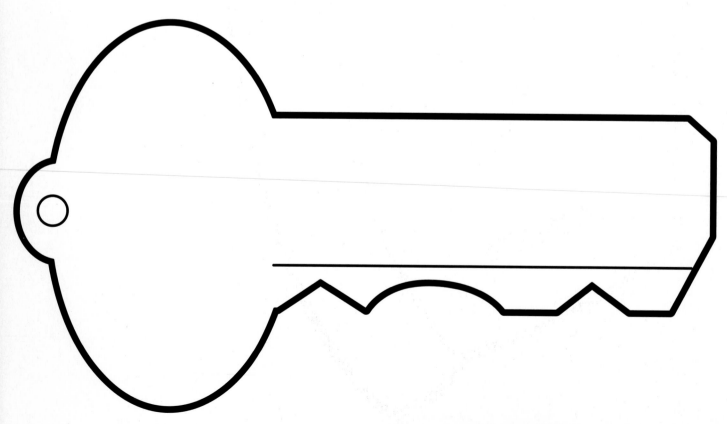

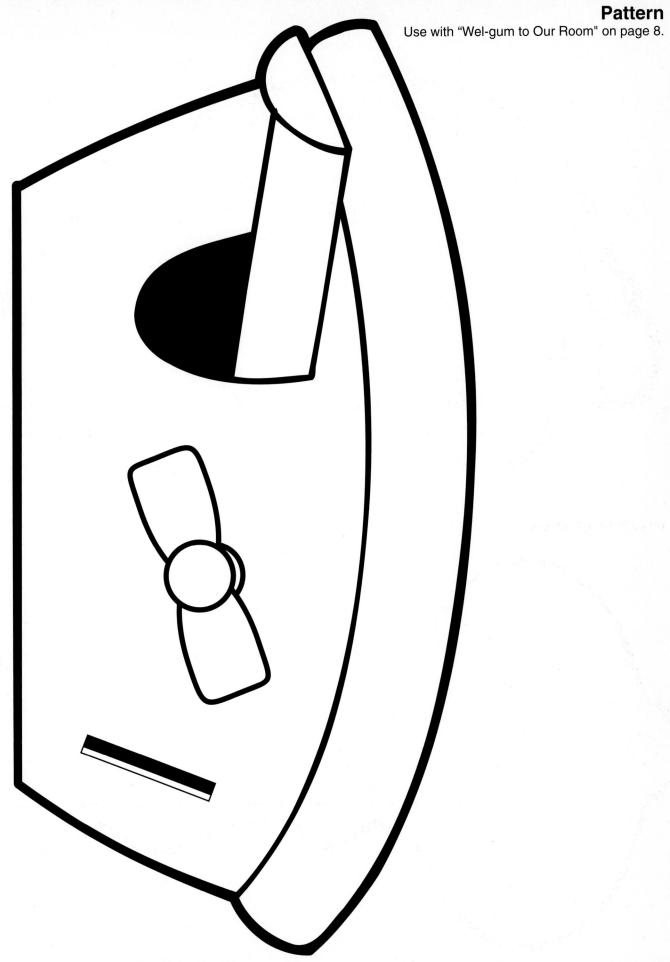

Use with "We're Bananas About School" on page 9.

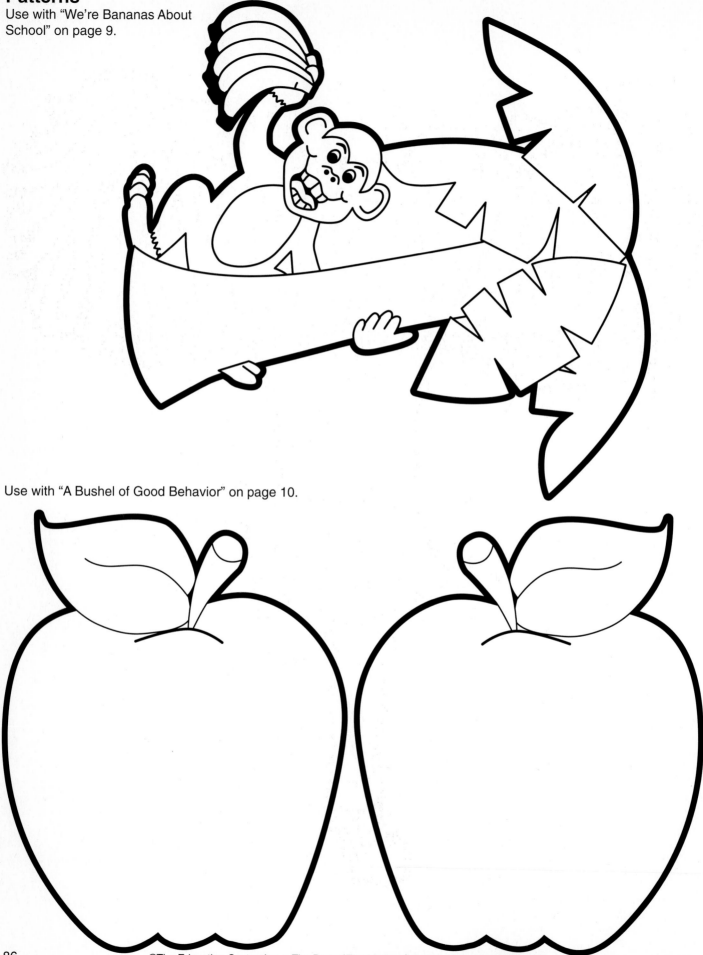

Use with "A Bushel of Good Behavior" on page 10.

Pattern
Use with "Cursive Kickoff!" on page 11.

THE BEST

Patterns

Use with "We're Nuts About Our Grandparents!" on page 12.

Patterns

Use with "The Cream of the Crop!" on page 14.

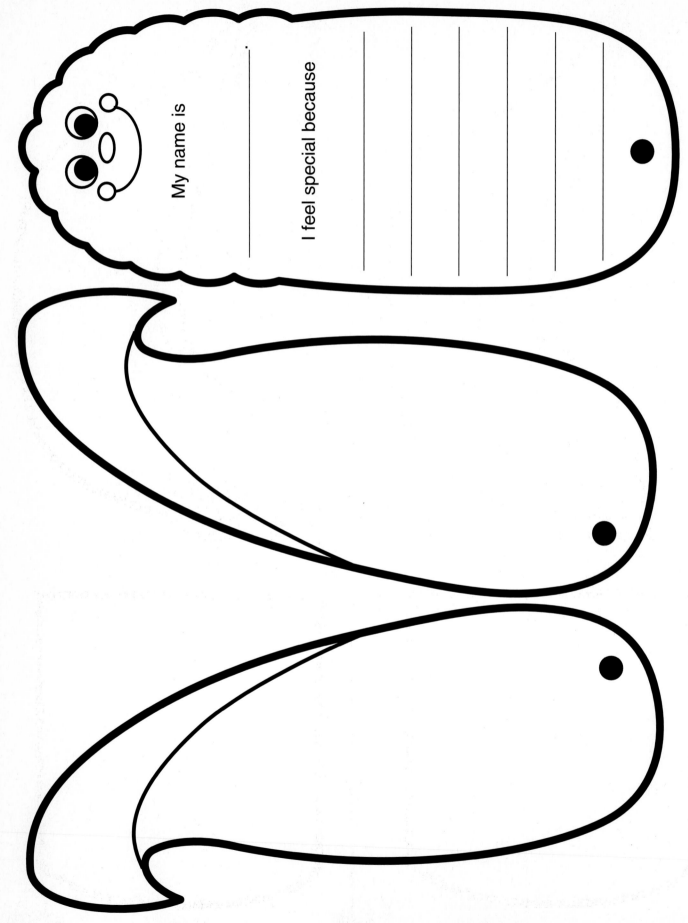

My name is

I feel special because

ship

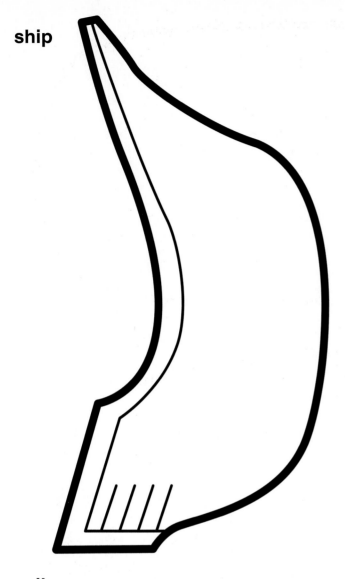

ship

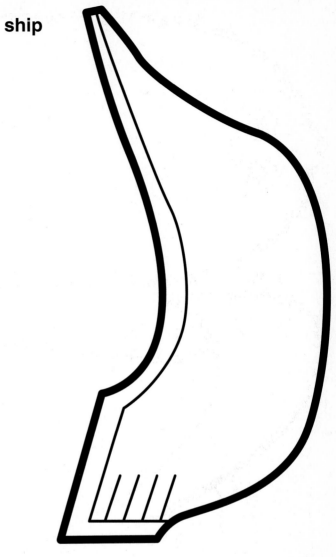

sail

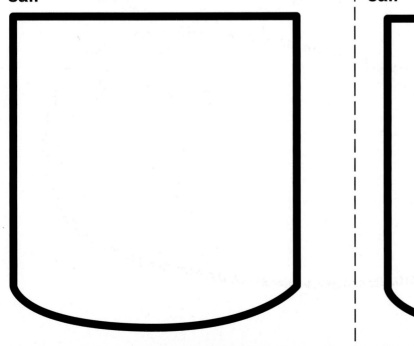

sail

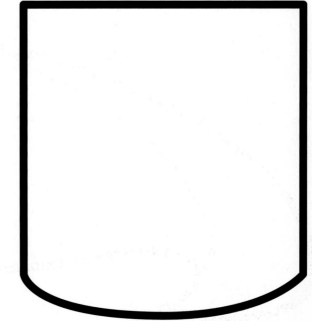

Pattern
Use with "Words Aren't Scary—Just Ask Your Dictionary!" on page 15.

Pattern

Use with "Gobblin' Great Spelling!" on page 16 and "Let's Talk Turkey!" on page 17.

Patterns

Use with "Gobblin' Great Spelling!" on page 16 and "Let's Talk Turkey!" on page 17.

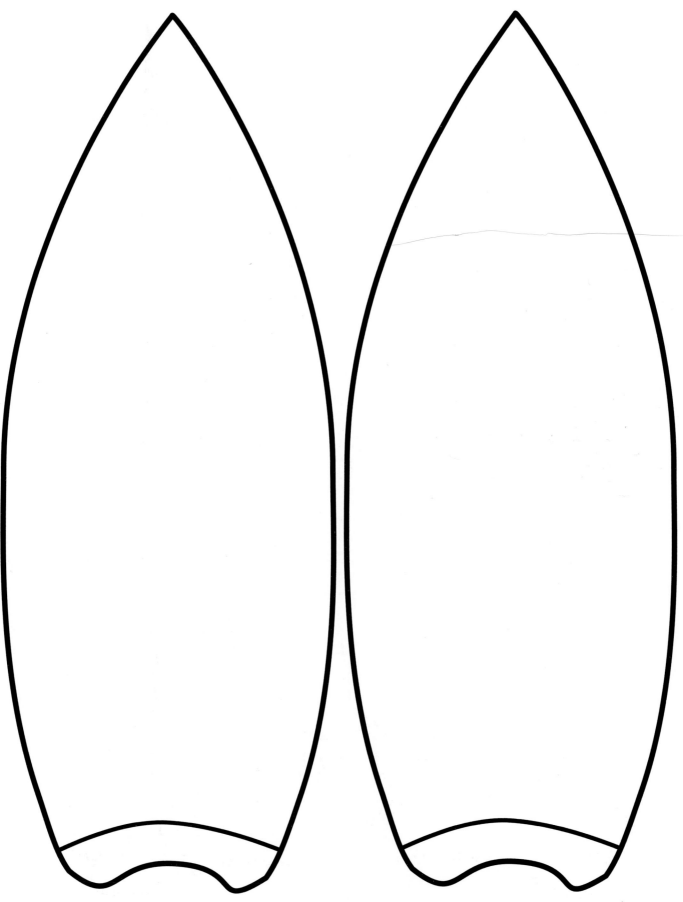

Pattern
Use with "We're Feasting on Books!" on page 17.

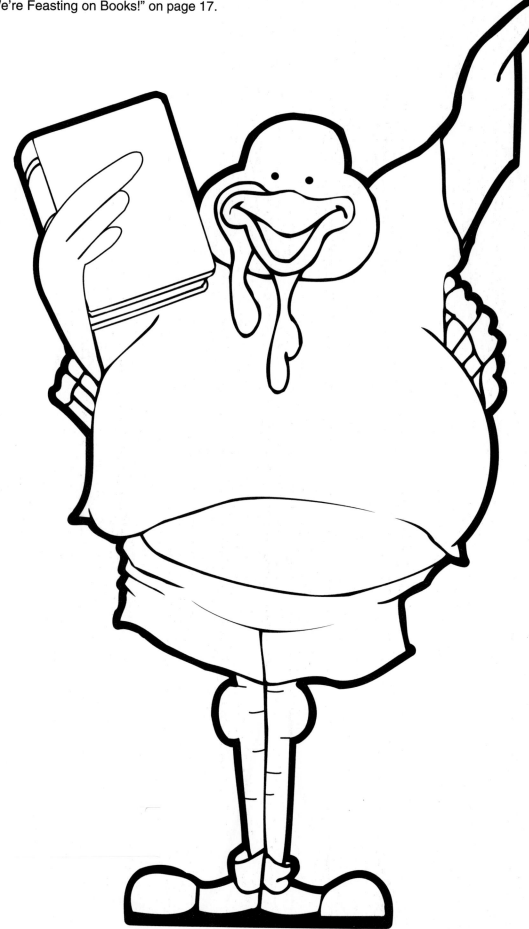

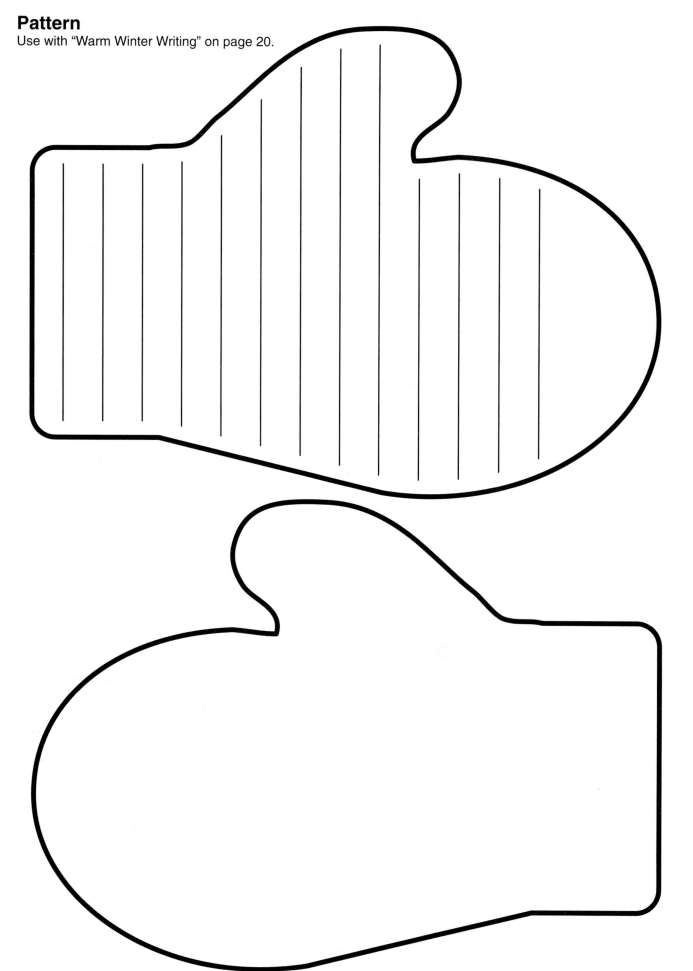

Pattern

Use with "Fashions for Frosty" on page 22.

Use with "Our Winter Wonderland" on page 22.

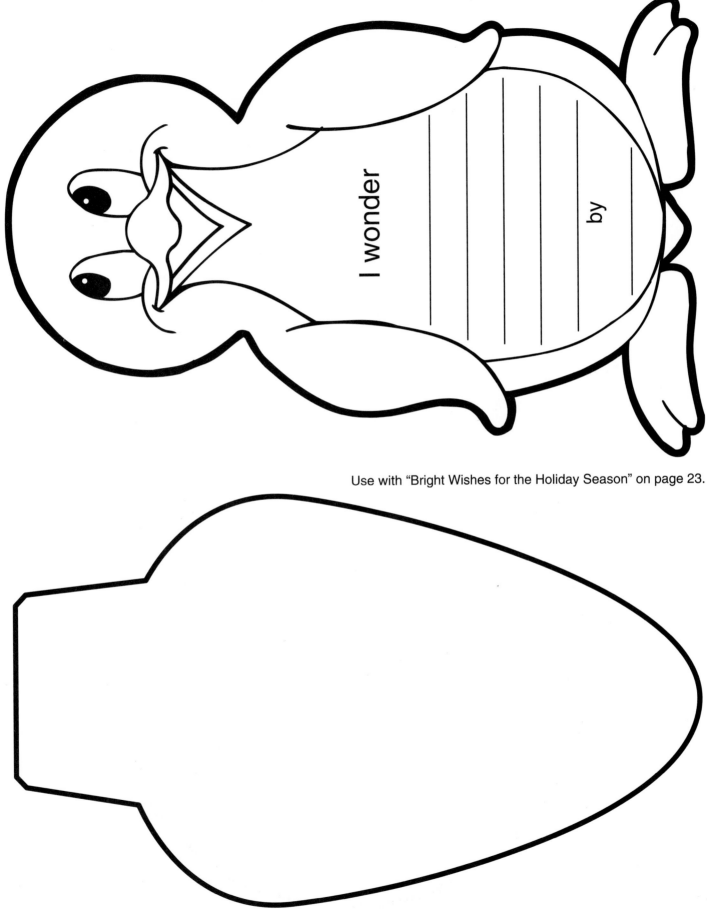

I wonder

by

Use with "Bright Wishes for the Holiday Season" on page 23.

Pattern

Use with "Snapshots of the Season" on page 23.

Pattern
Use with "Gifts of the
Season, Straight From
the Heart" on page 24.

Pattern and Awards

Use with "Rudolph's Challenge" on page 26.

I helped meet
Rudolph's challenge!

©The Education Center, Inc.

I helped meet
Rudolph's challenge!

©The Education Center, Inc.

Patterns

Use with "Happy Holidays!" on page 27, "Let the Stars Shine in 2004" on page 30, "Wanted! Reading Stars" on page 50, and "The Shining Stars of Second Grade" on page 63.

Use with "Not a Creature Was Stirring…Not Even a Mouse!" on page 28.

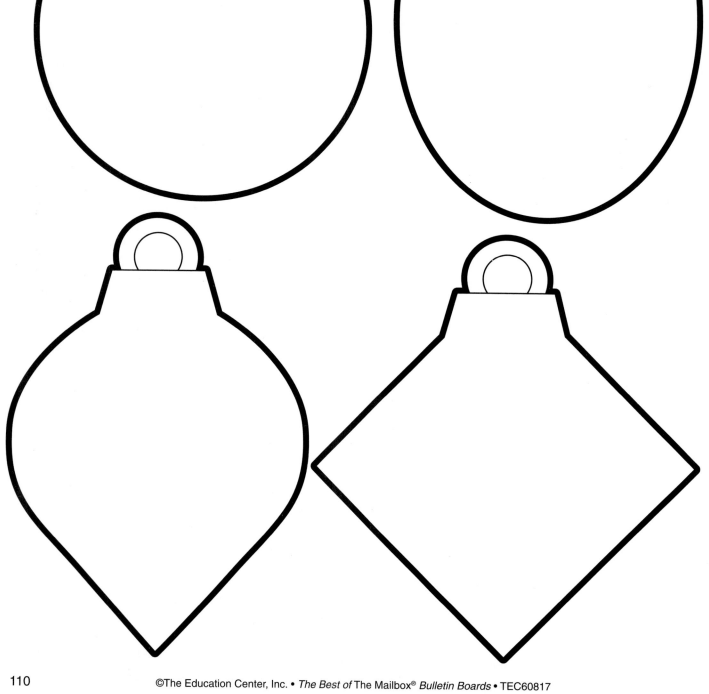

©The Education Center, Inc. • *The Best of* The Mailbox® *Bulletin Boards* • TEC60817

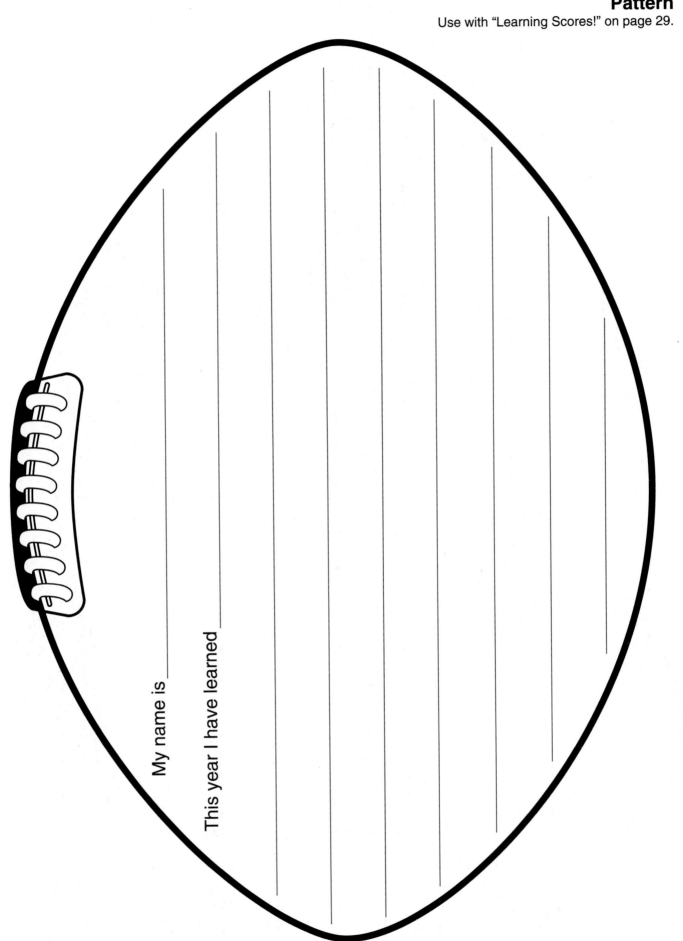

My name is _____

This year I have learned _____

Pattern
Use with "New Year Wishes" on page 30.

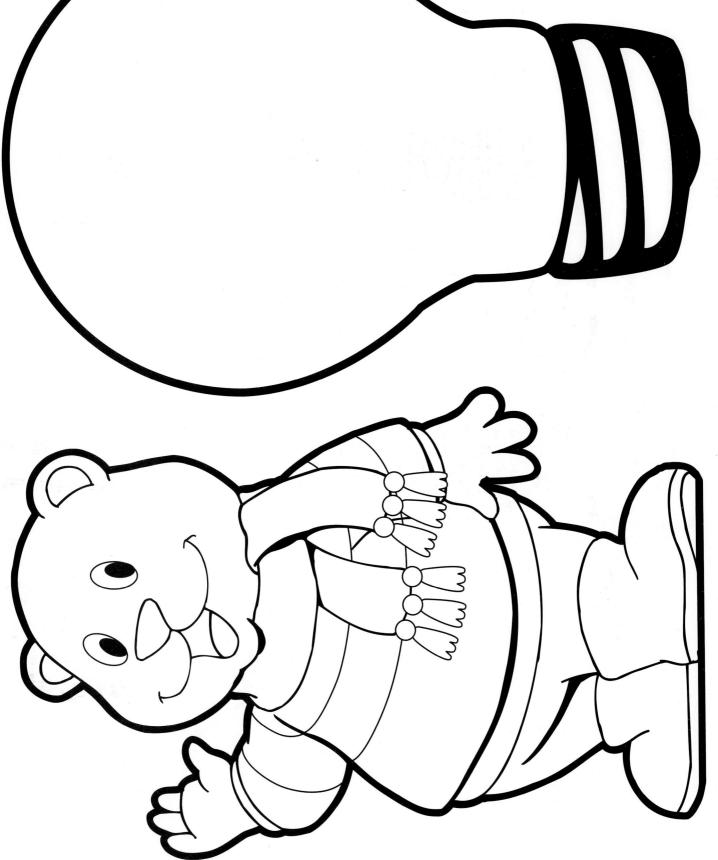

Pattern

Use with "Hats Off to a New Year!" on page 31.

HAPPY NEW YEAR

Patterns

Use the pot with "A Rainbow of Love" on page 34.

Use the heart with "Books Have
Captured Our Hearts!" and "A Rainbow
of Love" on page 34, and "Careers We
Love!" and "Our Wholehearted Ideas"
on page 37.

Pattern
Use with "Our Wholehearted Ideas" on page 37.

Patterns

Use with "Watching the Weather" on page 40.

Use with "A Rainbow of Reading" on page 41.

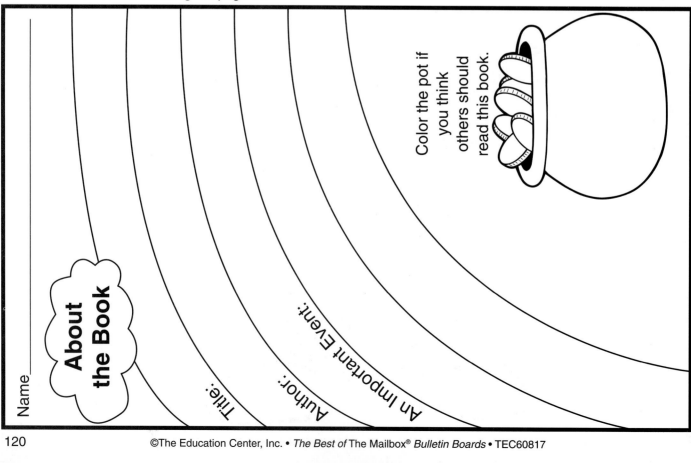

Pattern

Use with "Our Garden of Books" on page 42.

Patterns
Use with "We're Buzzing With Good Attendance" on page 43.

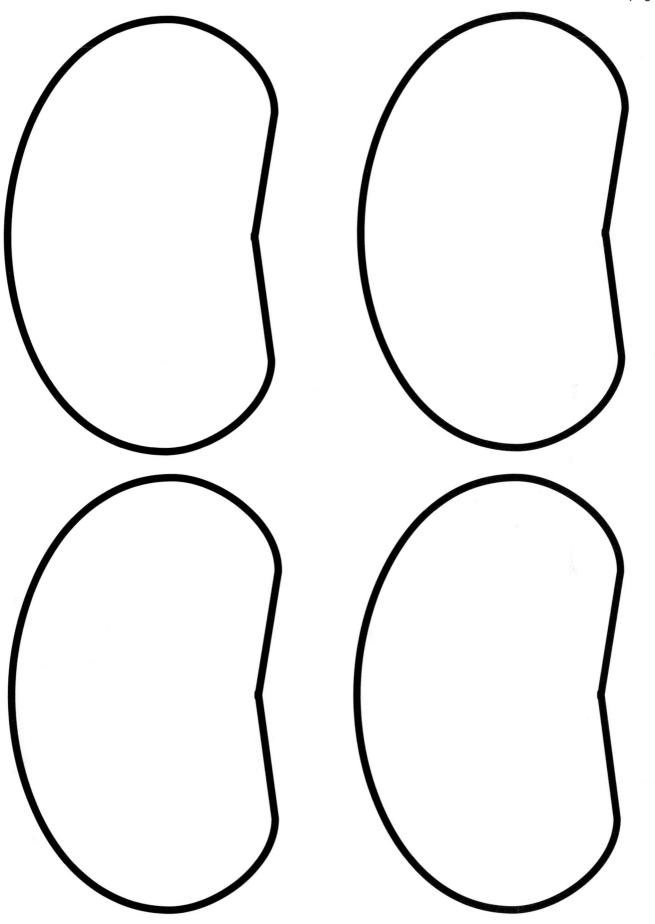

Patterns
Use with "Just Hatched!" on page 47.

Use with "On the Road With Recycling" on page 48.

Pattern

Use the berry patterns with "Our Work Is Nothing But the 'Berry' Best!" on page 49.

Pattern

Use with "Our Year Was out of This World!" on page 51.

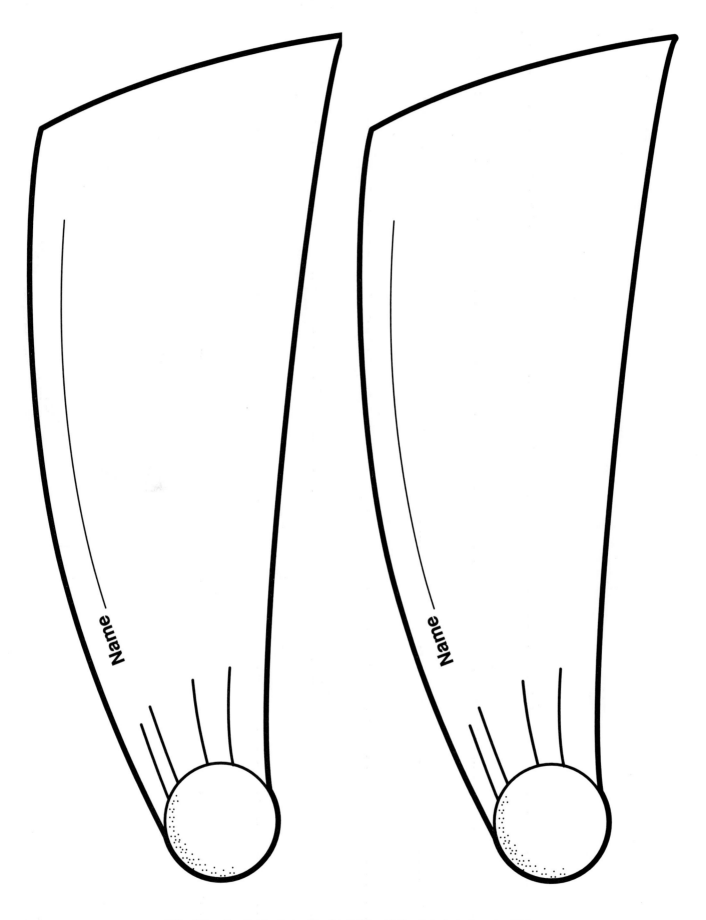

Name

Name

©The Education Center, Inc. • *The Best of* The Mailbox® *Bulletin Boards* • TEC60817

Pattern

Use with "Didn't the School Year Fly By?" on page 53.

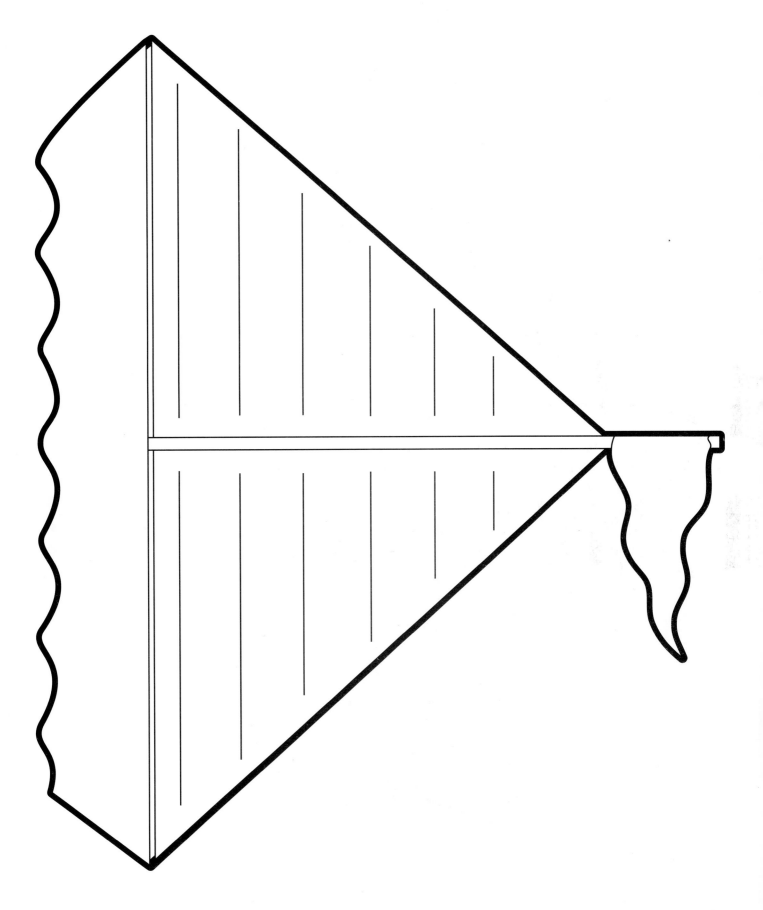

Pattern

Use with "This Year Has Been a Ball!" on page 55.

Use with "'Water' We Doing This Summer?" on page 56.

Pattern

Use with "Summertime Snapshots" on page 56.

Use with "Something to Talk About!" on page 59.

Patterns

Use with "Scenes From Second Grade!" on page 59.

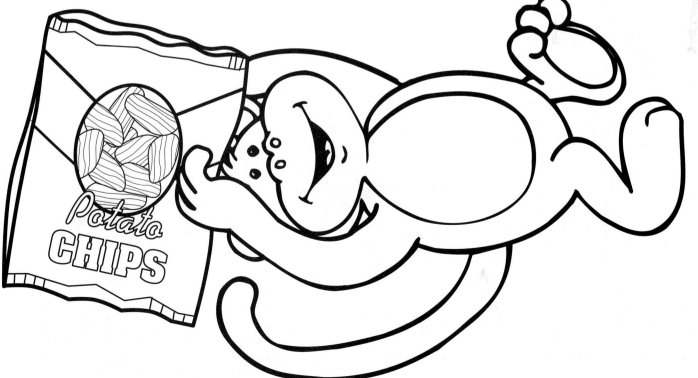

Patterns
Use with "Look Who Has Been Caught Being Kind!" on page 61.

Friendship Honey

Use with "Room 3's Busy Bees" on page 62.

Patterns

Use with "Help Wanted!" on page 62 and "We're Sharp!" on page 66.

Patterns

Use with "Working With This Class Is a Sweet Treat" on page 63.

Pattern

Use with "The Best in the West" on page 64.

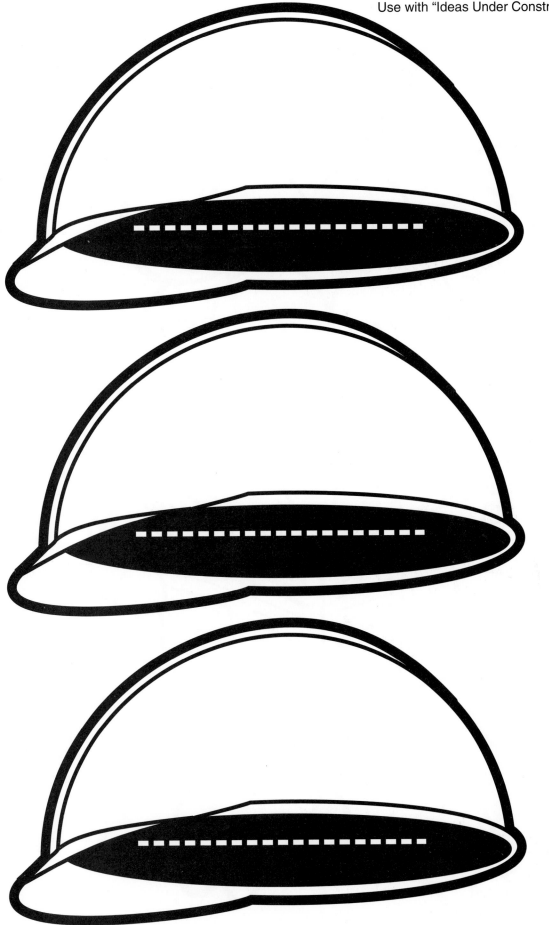

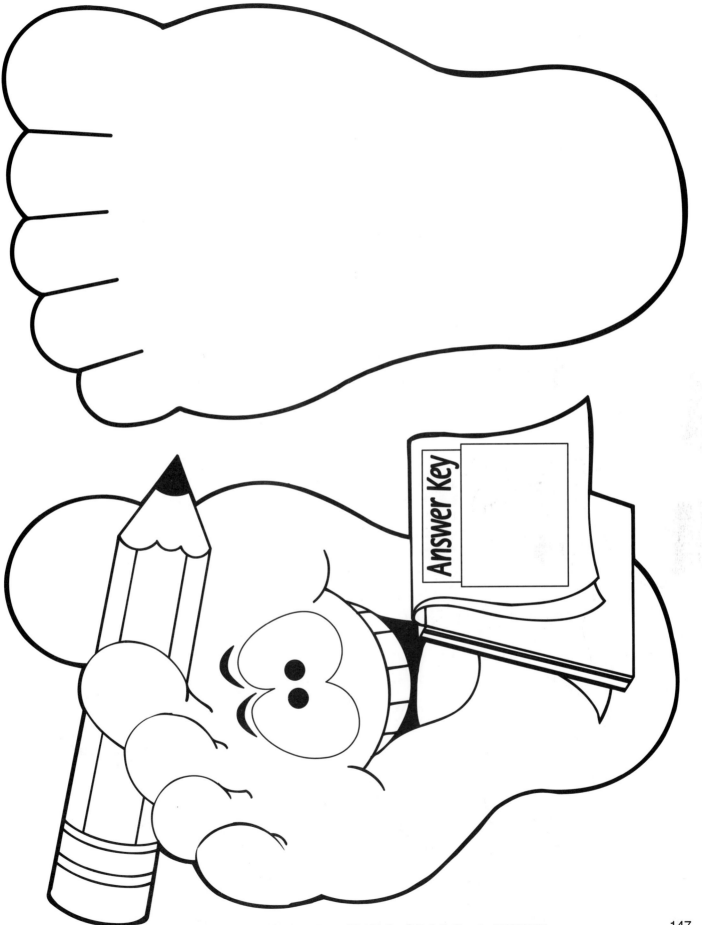

Answer Key

Patterns

Use with "Boning Up on Estimation" on page 67.

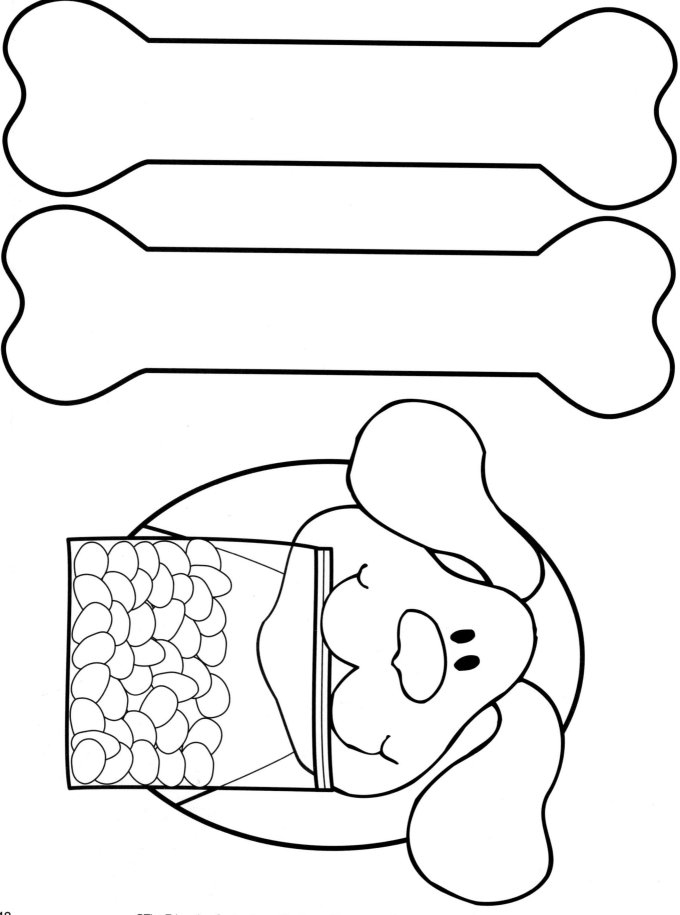

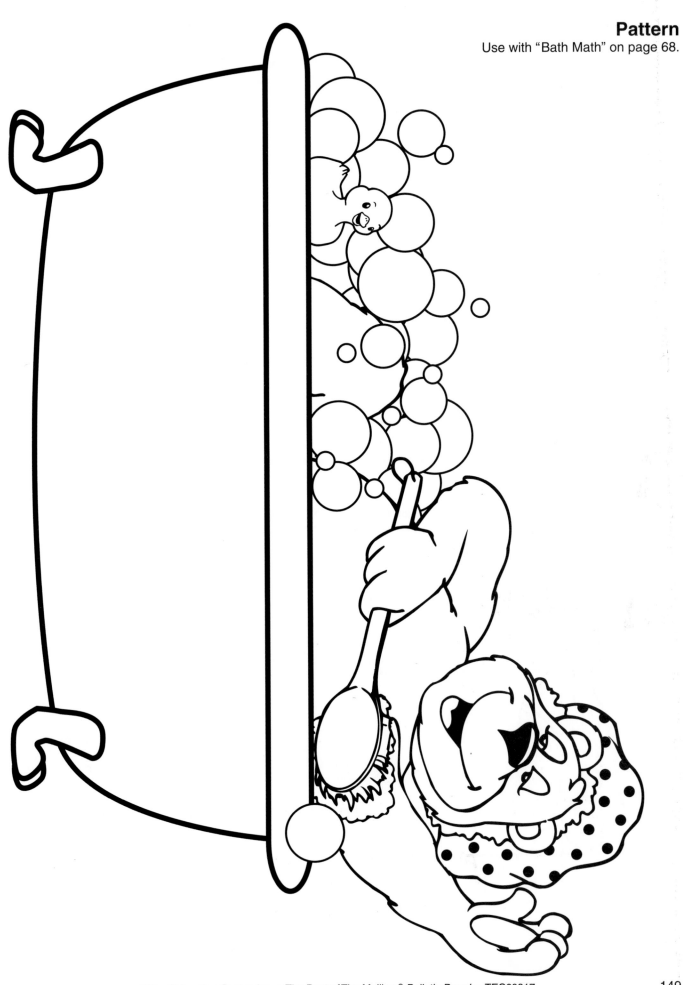

Patterns

Use with "Bumper-to-Bumper Facts" on page 68.

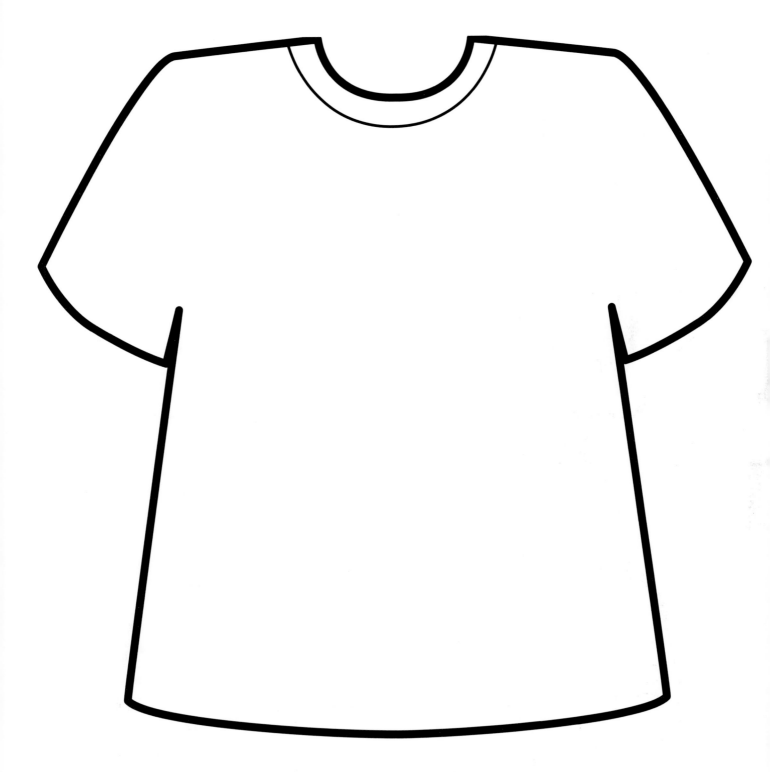

Pattern

Use with "Blast Off With Spelling!" on page 71.

NASA
United States

Patterns

Use with "We're Going Bananas Over Books!" on page 73.

Title: _____

Author: _____

To learn more about this book, ask

_____
(student)

This book was...
(check one)
○ Excellent
○ Good
○ O.K.

Use with "Get Your Paws on a Good Book!" on page 74.

Title ______________________________

Author ______________________________

This book was GREAT GOOD FAIR OK

I think you SHOULD/SHOULD NOT read this book because ______

____

____

____

Book reviewed by ______________________________

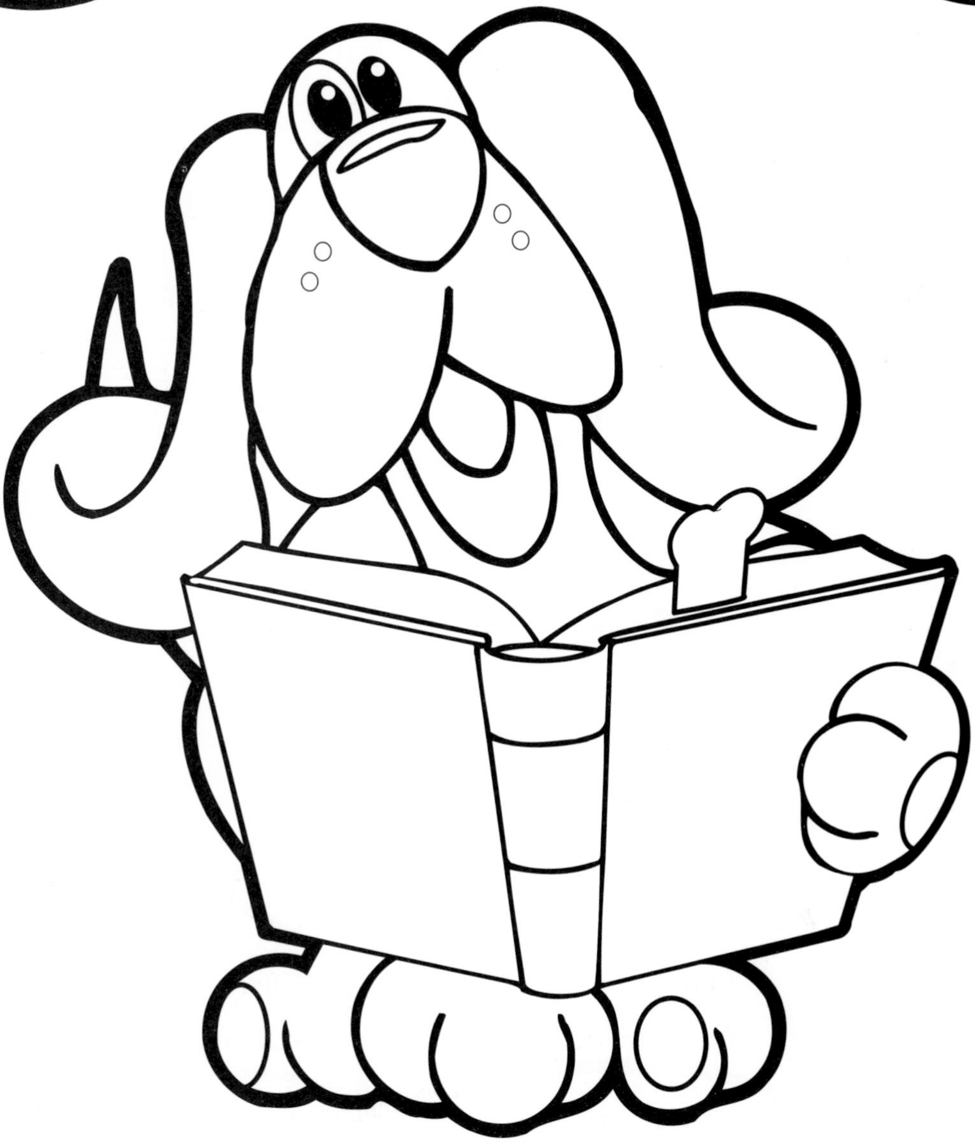

Pattern
Use with "Books Worth
Crowing About!" on page 75.

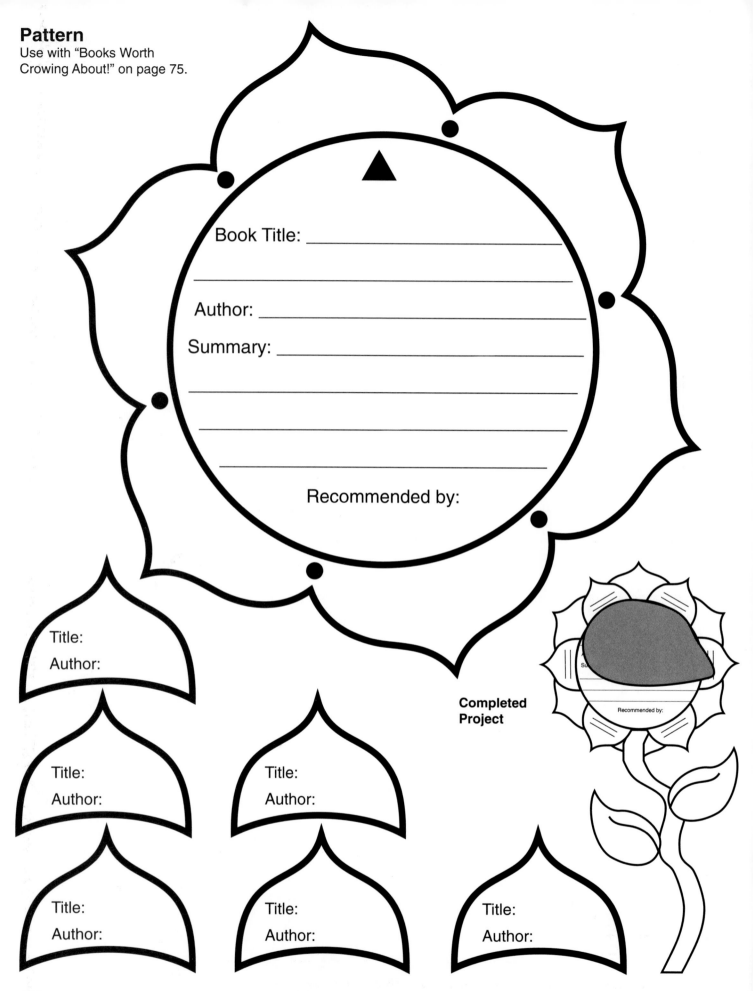

Book Title: _____

_____

Author: _____

Summary: _____

_____

_____

_____

Recommended by:

Title:
Author:

Title:
Author:

Title:
Author:

Title:
Author:

Title:
Author:

Title:
Author:

**Completed
Project**

Recommended by:

Pattern
Use with "We're Read-
ing 'Jean-iuses!'" on
page 76.

Name:

Date:

Title:

Author:

This book

Name:

Date:

Title:

Author:

This book

Patterns
Use with "Camera on the Community" on page 79.

Cut out.

Index